Data Protection Toolkit

Gill Steel
Rose Cottage
Woodman Lane
Sparsholt
Winchester
SO21 2NS

G.SWSE

E: gill.steel@lawskills.co.uk
T: 01962 776442

Related titles from Law Society Publishing:

Anti-Bribery Toolkit
Amy Bell

Anti-Money Laundering Toolkit
Alison Matthews

COFAs Toolkit
Jeremy Black and Florence Perret du Cray

COLPs Toolkit
Michelle Garlick

Lexcel Financial Management & Business Planning Toolkit
Law Society

Lexcel Information Management Toolkit (2nd edn)
Law Society

Outcomes-Focused Regulation
Andrew Hopper QC and Gregory Treverton-Jones QC

The Solicitor's Handbook 2013
Andrew Hopper QC and Gregory Treverton-Jones QC

Titles from Law Society Publishing can be ordered from all good bookshops or direct (telephone 0870 850 1422, email **lawsociety@prolog.uk.com** or visit our online shop at **bookshop.lawsociety. org.uk**).

Data Protection Toolkit

Alison Matthews

The Law Society

Crown copyright material is reproduced with the permission of the Controller of Her Majesty's Stationery Office

ISBN 978-1-907698-92-7

Published in 2014 by the Law Society
113 Chancery Lane, London WC2A 1PL

Typeset by Columns Design XML Ltd, Reading
Printed by TJ International Ltd, Padstow, Cornwall

The paper used for the text pages of this book is FSC® certified. FSC (the Forest Stewardship Council®) is an international network to promote responsible management of the world's forests.

FSC
www.fsc.org
MIX
Paper from
responsible sources
FSC® C013056

Contents

Foreword

While it is fair to say that many legal practices have been identifying and managing risks for a long time, the demands of the Legal Services Act 2007 and the Solicitors Regulation Authority's introduction of outcomes-focused regulation mean that all practices – whatever their shape, size or location – must prioritise risk management.

Instead of adhering to a precise set of rules the profession is now working toward a list of outcomes, supported by indicative behaviours, and this change in approach brings with it a greater focus on regulating the practice as well as the individual solicitor.

To help practices meet their legal and regulatory obligations, the Law Society established its Risk and Compliance Service. To date, the Service's compliance support offering includes bespoke in-house consultancy, webinars, monthly e-newsletters, master classes, seminars and conferences.

It is important for solicitors to be aware that they will not need to re-work all their systems and procedures in the light of the SRA Code of Conduct 2011. This is particularly pertinent for sole practitioners, who are often the senior partner, law firm manager and risk professional rolled into one.

With these things in mind, the Law Society's Risk and Compliance Service in collaboration with a number of subject matter experts has commissioned this series of hands-on toolkits.

These practical guides have been prepared with the busy practitioner in mind. They aim to help reduce the cost of compliance for practitioners by providing a useful set of reference notes, definitions, best practice tips and templates. Much of their content is informed by first-hand information gleaned through onsite risk diagnostic visits and interactions with members of the profession, and in response to practitioner requests for tools to assist in their compliance journey.

Our hope is that these toolkits rapidly become 'must-have' elements in every practitioner's compliance armoury and to this end I recommend them to you without reservation.

The Risk and Compliance Service would like to thank the author, Alison Matthews, for her contribution to the *Data Protection Toolkit*.

Pearl Moses
Lead Consultant: Risk and Compliance
Law Society Consulting
The Law Society

Preface

Solicitors and their employees are familiar with their duty to keep clients' affairs confidential, but outcome 7.5 of the SRA Code of Conduct 2011 (the SRA Code) also requires solicitors to comply with the data protection legislation, the Data Protection Act 1998 (DPA). Information security may be seen as a separate issue, and it is important to note that information is broader than data as defined by the DPA. However, by putting systems in place to comply with the DPA, legal practices should ensure that they meet the obligations in chapter 4 of the SRA Code and those systems should help to keep information secure, a challenging issue given the increase in cybercrime.

Legal practices should review whether they are complying with their obligations now given the business risks of non-compliance and with the prospect of the EU Data Protection Regulation being finalised during 2014 and coming into force 12/24 months later. Legal practices with robust and effective systems and controls will find it easier to build on them to meet the more onerous requirements of the Data Protection Regulation.

Legal practices hold a wide range of data in a variety of different ways. Not only do practices hold client data, but they also hold data about employees and third parties. It is held electronically and on a range of devices. Most legal practices will still handle data in paper form, whether on client files or other paper systems or simply sending letters and attachments in the post.

A legal practice must ensure that, however the data is held, it is held securely. With the increase in the volume of data held, this is a significant challenge.

While the DPA focuses on data held electronically, it is important to be aware that data held in a 'relevant filing system' is also subject to the DPA. If a legal practice operates a highly efficient manual filing system in which records relating to individuals are held in a sufficiently systematic, structured way as to allow ready access to specific information about those individuals, that is likely to be a 'relevant filing system'. Reference is made to the definition at **1.4.1** and the Information Commissioner's Office's (ICO's) FAQs.

Even if the data is not held in a 'relevant filing system', legal practices must still ensure that data or client information held in paper format is also kept secure, for example, a legal practice must send a letter enclosing medical records to the right client at the right address.

In certain circumstances serious contraventions of the Act, which may involve a failure to keep data secure, can result in a maximum fine of £500,000 from the ICO, disciplinary action from the SRA, complaints from clients and criticism from the Legal Ombudsman (LeO).

This toolkit refers to personal data and to information depending on the context. Personal data is defined by the DPA (see **1.4.1**). Client information has a wider meaning and covers all the information held about a client, which must be kept confidential. Legal practices need to understand the distinction and to be clear what constitutes personal data such that the DPA applies and what is client information, subject to confidentiality.

This toolkit is designed to accompany the Law Society's practice notes on data protection, confidentiality and information security and the *Lexcel Information Management Toolkit* (2nd edition, Law Society, 2013). It aims to provide solicitors with practical assistance to implement effective systems and procedures to demonstrate compliance with their regulatory obligations. The ICO's website is also a valuable resource for legal practices (**www.ico.org.uk**).

Why have written procedures?

Written procedures will help your managers/partners, owners and employees to understand what is expected of them and so enable your practice to demonstrate to regulators that you are complying with your legal and regulatory obligations. Written procedures will also reduce the risk of your practice breaching confidentiality or the DPA and therefore minimise the risks of regulatory, criminal or civil sanctions.

How to use this toolkit

Legal practices are not required to use this toolkit, but may find it a useful reference tool to assess the quality and coverage of their own procedures. Regardless of how your legal practice chooses to use the toolkit, each practice should assess its risks and review and adapt the policies and procedures to fit the needs of the practice, particularly as many contain options for compliance. The risk-based approach means that legal practices should ensure that their systems work for their business model, taking account of the risks faced by them. There is no value in implementing systems that are difficult to use and the support of managers/partners and employees is vital to the effective implementation and maintenance of good data protection systems. Employees need to understand why compliance with the DPA is important and what the risks of non-compliance are.

Legal practices may choose to use the toolkit by either:

- using some or all of the procedures and forms so their data protection systems are integrated with their other business and regulatory procedures; or
- implementing stand-alone data protection procedures which simply refer to other policies.

All of the draft procedures and forms in the toolkit are provided as Word documents on the accompanying CD-Rom. Simply purchasing this toolkit and putting it on a shelf will be insufficient to demonstrate to regulators that your legal practice has data protection policies and procedures which are appropriate for your practice.

You may decide that certain procedures or forms suggested in the toolkit are not appropriate for your legal practice, but consider what purpose they are designed to meet before deleting them.

Further assistance in meeting your obligations is available through the Law Society's Risk and Compliance Service (see **www.lawsociety.org.uk/riskandcompliance**).

Abbreviations

AML	anti-money laundering
CDD	client due diligence
COFA	compliance officer for finance and administration
COLP	compliance officer for legal practice
CPD	continuing professional development
DBIS	Department for Business, Innovation & Skills
DP	data protection
DPA	Data Protection Act 1998
DP officer	data protection officer
EEA	European Economic Area
ICO	Information Commissioner's Office
LeO	Legal Ombudsman
MLRO	money laundering reporting officer
OFR	outcomes-focused regulation
PECR	Privacy and Electronic Communications (EC Directive) Regulations 2003 (SI 2003/2426)
PI	personal injury
SAR	subject access request
SRA	Solicitors Regulation Authority

Abbreviations

PART 1
Setting the scene

This section of the toolkit considers how senior management can ensure their legal practice has appropriate and risk-based systems to protect personal data, maintain confidentiality and keep information secure.

1 Setting up systems

1.1 Overview

If a legal practice fails to have robust systems and controls in place to comply with the Data Protection Act 1998 (DPA) and the SRA Code of Conduct 2011 (the SRA Code), it faces a range of regulatory sanctions, financial penalties and reputational consequences. As a result, not only does a practice need good systems and controls but it needs a culture (set by senior management) in which everyone understands the importance of data protection compliance, client confidentiality and information security.

Those systems need to be clear, practical, commercial, user friendly and relevant to the legal practice. A personal injury practice must protect medical records (sensitive personal data) and ensure that expert witnesses return medical records securely or destroy the data securely at the end of a matter. A commercial practice must protect the financial records and intellectual property of a client company. The systems that the legal practice needs to have in place are likely to be different, depending on the data held, the client and the nature of the work.

All employees from the most junior office assistant to the IT support as well as the client-facing employees need to understand the basic concepts of confidentiality, data protection and information security. Legal practices must ensure that employees understand that the following are all breaches of confidentiality/data protection:

- Telling someone that the practice is acting for a well-known footballer.
- Talking about a client's matter in the lift or on the train.
- Leaving a laptop, Blackberry or a client file on the train.
- Enclosing the wrong attachment with a letter or email.

To comply with the DPA and the eight data protection principles, the legal practice's systems will need to cover:

- appointment of a data protection officer (see **1.3**);
- registration with the Information Commissioner's Office (ICO) (see **1.5**);
- identification and management of data (**Chapter 2**);
- fair and lawful processing of data (**Chapter 3**);
- accuracy of data (**Chapters 3** and **4**);
- access to data (**Chapter 5**);
- data security (**Chapter 5**);
- relations with third parties (**Chapter 6**);
- dealing with subject access requests (SARs) (**Chapter 7**);
- complaints handling (**Chapter 8**);
- data retention/destruction (**Chapter 9**);
- training (**Chapter 10**);
- monitoring (**Chapter 11**).

As with anti-money laundering (AML), the obligations can be daunting and it can be challenging to know where to start and how to keep control of how data is handled. The powers of the ICO to levy fines of up to £500,000 and to 'name and shame' are such that legal practices do need to invest the time and resources to 'get it right'. This toolkit is designed to help legal practices achieve this.

As with AML, it is not just a case of implementing effective policies and procedures; it is also necessary to have a good compliance culture in which employees understand their obligations, are committed to complying with those obligations and are focused on helping to resolve issues of concern. A strong culture of compliance and good risk management are critical for success in meeting the challenges of outcomes-focused regulation (OFR).

In addition, clients, particularly corporate clients, may have very specific requirements about how data is to be shared and handled, how a legal practice can demonstrate that data is held securely and how any breaches must be notified not only to the client but also to the ICO.

The degree of management commitment and engagement (which is likely to be led by or at least involve the compliance officer for legal practice (COLP)) will determine success or failure. Legal practices should allocate day-to-day responsibility for data protection to an individual with appropriate authority to be the data protection (DP) officer. The DP officer needs to liaise closely with the COLP to ensure that data protection compliance is properly managed, e.g. data protection is on the risk register and breaches/incidents are recorded and followed up. The appointment makes it clear to the practice that data protection compliance is an important issue.

It is important to note the following:

- 'Management board' (the board) means the legal practice's governance structure, whether that is the sole practitioner, two partners who run the legal practice or an elected board as required by outcome 7.1 of the SRA Code.
- Legal practices will have different approaches to business support functions depending on their size, but IT, accounts/finance, HR and marketing personnel may be able to provide valuable assistance and support.
- Legal practices should consider the points in each chapter and apply them in a risk-based and proportionate way given their risk profile, particularly their size, type of work and clients.

1.2 Management commitment

Legal practices should now be familiar with the concept of creating a compliance culture, although they may be unsure how to achieve that. Compliance should, with the advent of COLPs and compliance officers for finance and administration (COFAs), now be at the top of the management board agenda (together with strategy/revenue), with clear messages being sent to the practice that non-compliance is not an option. A good compliance culture has to be led from the top.

Data protection affects every part of the legal practice: not only the client-facing teams but also the business support functions, IT, marketing, HR and finance as well as the risk/compliance function. The impact on the practice of inadequate compliance in this field is significant and therefore it is vital that there is a board level (or equivalent) champion who has the management authority to ensure that the data protection obligations are complied with by everyone in the practice and ensures that there are sufficient resources and support available to the practice.

In some practices, it may be the DP officer who has that overall responsibility; in others, the DP officer may be the technical expert with the COLP having the management authority and who ensures that the DP officer's advice is taken into account by the business support functions and the client-facing areas.

It does need to be made clear to all employees that this data protection training must be completed, that data protection breaches will be treated seriously and that queries must be raised at the earliest opportunity as this enables the legal practice to mitigate the risks and minimise any reputational consequences.

The business support functions are critical to the success of an effective data protection compliance regime, as follows:

- IT will tend to oversee some technical aspects of information security as well as the day-to-day computer and electronic systems and ensure that the practice is protected against cybercrime. There should be close liaison with the DP officer to ensure systems are effective, integrated, compatible and backed up.
- The marketing/business development function needs to manage the reputational consequences of any significant data loss, ensure the client database contains the minimum information, e.g. no sensitive personal data and that direct marketing is compliant with the regulatory obligations.
- The accounts/finance team will ensure the financial systems/records are robust and secure to minimise the risk of fraud, for both clients and the legal practice.
- HR will ensure that appropriate action is taken for breaches of policy/procedure, employee data is properly protected, compliance is built into the training/ induction programme and the annual appraisal/promotion process.

The board needs to be advised of major issues that could have reputational consequences, e.g. potential referrals to the ICO or potential press interest but given the importance of the issue, there should be a regular update on the board agenda. A detailed annual report to the board will provide an assessment of the adequacy of the legal practice's systems as a management tool as well as showing the regulators that data protection rusks are being property managed.

Managers/partners will make sure that their teams are properly trained in the systems and procedures, that issues of concern are properly addressed and raised with the DP officer, incidents reported and that appropriate action is taken where there is non-compliance.

Responsibility for ensuring that the systems are effective and workable rests with all partners/managers but the DP officer, the board and the COLP will ensure that the legal practice is meeting its data protection obligations fully.

Identifying the right person to appoint as the DP officer enables the board and the COLP to have confidence that day-to-day compliance is being properly managed.

1.3 The data protection officer

While there is no legal requirement to appoint a DP officer, the ICO does ask, at registration, if there is someone responsible for ensuring compliance with the DPA. In addition, it is difficult to see how the legal practice will ensure compliance with the legislation as required by outcome 7.5 of the SRA Code, without appointing someone with specific responsibility.

Significant challenges for legal practices include being able to deal with subject access requests (SARs) and dealing with data security/loss issues if mistakes are made. Legal practices also need to ensure day-to-day compliance with the DPA, confidentiality and information security obligations.

By having a DP officer with overall responsibility for compliance, a legal practice should ensure there are effective policies and procedures, as well as a consistent approach and one person to whom queries and SARs can be directed.

Appointing the right person as the DP officer is critical. Many firms will appoint a person already responsible for compliance with other regulatory obligations as he or she should understand the principles of good compliance. The individual does need sufficient seniority, technical expertise and the ability to command respect, have access to files and other information, and a good understanding of a complex area of law to enable him or her to:

- convince the board, the managers/partners and employees to take DP/information security compliance seriously;
- give clear, practical and commercial guidance;
- make appropriate and considered decisions;
- ensure that robust systems, controls and procedures are in place;
- arrange for relevant employees to have relevant training;
- identify whether to report to the ICO and manage liaison with the ICO and, where appropriate, a client/data controller/data processor on any report or other matter.

In making the decision as to who to appoint, the board should bear in mind that the DP officer may have to deal with subject access requests from current or former employees, who may be (or be about to be) in dispute with the practice. The DP officer will need to be able to work closely with HR in what may be challenging circumstances.

The main responsibilities of a DP officer are to:

- familiarise him or herself with the DPA, guidance and relevant case law and keep up to date with any changes;
- register the business with the ICO, keep the registration up to date and renew it annually;
- advise on potential data protection incidents in liaison with the COLP;
- regularly 'audit' the practice's use of personal data and check to ensure compliance;
- draw up a written data protection policy which all employees are required to be aware of, understand and comply with;
- advise on the data protection implications of new products/services and new information security/IT systems and procedures;
- liaise with managers/partners/employees;
- liaise with data controllers/processors;
- liaise with/report to the ICO;
- ensure that subject access requests and other legitimate DPA requests are handled in accordance with the appropriate timescales in a timely manner.

Whether the DP officer is a solicitor or partner/manager, the DP officer needs to have the support of the board so that he or she is credible. Even if an individual is given responsibility for data protection in a practice, he or she will be acting on behalf of the practice, which will be the data controller.

Once the DP officer is appointed, it would be prudent to have stability and consistency of approach so a two-year appointment may be sensible. The legal practice and the DP officer should consider succession planning so there is a seamless transition at the appropriate time. Appointing an assistant would ensure that there is cover for absences.

While the DP officer will have primary responsibility (although not personal liability like the money laundering reporting officer (MLRO), the board, the COLP and the managers/partners also have regulatory obligations under chapter 7 of the SRA Code and the DPA. They can be subject to disciplinary and criminal sanctions and the legal practice can face fines of up to £500,000 from the ICO.

The board must ensure that the DP officer is properly supported and resourced, including the provision of systems, e.g. IT as well as sufficient support for the size and risk profile of the legal practice.

The DP officer must keep up to date with the legislation and any changes by attending seminars and networking groups, undertaking training and reading relevant journals and updates from the SRA, the Law Society, the ICO and other relevant associations.

Depending on the size of the legal practice, further support may be needed from a compliance assistant, who needs to be properly trained and supported.

The DP officer and deputy DP officer (and, where relevant, the compliance assistant/team) must be accessible, approachable, pragmatic, commercial, supportive and sympathetic to ensure employees and managers/partners feel comfortable asking him or her for guidance, sometimes in difficult or sensitive circumstances.

The DP officer and deputy DP officer need to be familiar with the key principles of the DPA and the definitions, which are considered in the next section.

1.4 Key principles

The DPA regulates the processing of personal data and implements the Data Protection Directive in the UK. (A new Data Protection Regulation is expected to be adopted by the European Parliament during 2014 and is likely to come into force in member states in 2016. The provisions are expected to be more onerous.)

The DPA protects the rights of individuals (data subjects) about whom 'personal data' is held mainly by placing duties on those who decide how and why such data is processed (data controllers). Not only is it important to understand the key terms but it is also important to understand the difference between data controllers and data processors as they are treated differently under the DPA.

Legal practices and their employees should already be familiar with the eight data protection principles (see DPA, Sched.1) which are set out in full at **Annex 1D**. The requirements are that personal data will:

- be obtained fairly and lawfully and not be processed unless certain conditions are met;
- be obtained for a specific and lawful purpose and not be processed in a manner which is incompatible with such purpose or purposes;
- be adequate, relevant and not excessive;
- be accurate and kept up to date;
- not be held longer than necessary;
- be processed in accordance with the rights of data subjects;
- be subject to appropriate security measures;
- not be transferred outside the European Economic Area (EEA), except in certain circumstances.

There are clear links between the second principle (the 'purpose limitation' principle) and other data protection principles: for example, if you obtain data for an unlawful purpose, you will breach the first principle as well as the second principle. Therefore, it is important to be clear why data is being collected and what it will be used for as this will help to comply with the other principles. If you wish to use or disclose the data for an additional or different purpose, you will need to ensure that the new use or disclosure is fair. You also need to ensure that you provide privacy notices to clients when collecting data and that the legal practice is registered with the ICO.

1.4.1 Key definitions

1. **Data** broadly means information which is held electronically or is part of a 'relevant filing system' or forms part of an accessible record (the latter will not generally be relevant to solicitors).
2. **Personal data** – data which relates to a living individual who can be identified from that data, or from that data and other information which is in the possession of, or is likely to come into the possession of, the data controller, and includes any expression of opinion about the individual and any indication of the intentions of the data controller or any other person in respect of the individual.
3. **Sensitive personal data** – means personal data consisting of data as to:

    (a) racial or ethnic origin of the data subject;
    (b) political opinions;
    (c) religious beliefs or similar beliefs;
    (d) trade union membership;
    (e) physical or mental health or condition;
    (f) sexual life;
    (g) the commission or alleged commission of any offence; or
    (h) any proceedings for any offence committed or alleged to have been committed, the disposal of such proceedings or the sentence of any court in such proceedings.

4. **Processing** is widely defined and it is difficult to think of anything an organisation might do with data that cannot be defined as processing.
5. **Data subject** means a living individual who is the subject of personal data.
6. **Data controller** means a person (usually an organisation) who (alone or jointly or in common with other persons) determines the purposes for which and the manner in which any personal data is, or is to be, processed. However, two or more persons (usually organisations) can be joint data controllers where they act together to decide the purpose and manner of any data processing. The term 'in common' applies where two or more persons share a pool of personal data that they process independently of each other.
7. **Data processor** – in relation to personal data, means any person (other than an employee of the data controller) who processes the data on behalf of the data controller.
8. **Relevant filing system** broadly relates to non-automated records that are structured in a way which allows ready access to information about individuals. The ICO's FAQs provide further guidance (**http://ico.org.uk/for_organisations/ guidance_index/~/media/documents/library/Data_Protection/Detailed_ specialist_guides/relevant_filing_systems_faqs.ashx**) following the decision in *Durant* v. *FSA* [2003] EWCA Civ 1746. This definition is particularly relevant for subject access requests (see **Chapter 7**).
9. **Third party** – in relation to personal data, means any person other than the data subject, the data controller or the data processor or other person authorised to process data for the data controller or processor.

As a legal practice you will be processing personal data, some of which will be sensitive, so you need to register your legal practice with the ICO.

1.5 Registration

New practices will need to register before starting to practise; existing legal practices should already be registered with the ICO. Failure to notify the ICO if you are processing data is a criminal offence and solicitors have been fined because of this. If the legal practice owns any separate businesses, those businesses are likely to need to be registered in their own right.

Legal practices will be data controllers, because the practice will determine how the data is used. Individuals within the practice will be processing the data on behalf of the legal practice. Legal practices will receive personal data and sensitive personal data from a range of data subjects, particularly clients and employees, as well as third parties.

1.5.1 How to register

The registration form can be downloaded from **www.ico.org.uk/for_organisations/ data_protection/registration/data-protection-registration**. The document can be completed, saved electronically as a PDF, attached to an email and sent back to the ICO.

Once you indicate your sector (i.e. legal) and nature of work as solicitor/legal services, there is a standard list of data subjects, recipients, purposes, etc. If you process data for additional reasons, for example, CCTV for crime prevention or providing financial services, you will need to confirm that is the case. You will also be asked whether you transfer data outside the European Economic Area (EEA), this will be relevant if you have clients based in non-EEA jurisdictions, due to the eighth data protection principle.

You will need to indicate who is responsible for data protection in your practice and how you will meet your obligations under the DPA. The fee is £35 unless you have more than 249 employees and a turnover of more than £25.9 million, in which case it is £500.

Once the ICO has checked your application and you have agreed the register entry, your legal practice will appear on the register. You will be given a security number and a registration number.

You are likely to be asked by third parties whether your legal practice is registered with the ICO and what your number is, so make sure your employees know where to access the information. You will need to renew your registration every year but the ICO will remind you and renewal is almost automatic if you pay by direct debit.

1.6 Policies and procedures

A legal practice's policies and procedures should provide employees with all the information they need to comply with the regulatory obligations. They should also set out the board's commitment to effective and robust data protection controls and the responsibilities of all employees of the legal practice.

As data controllers, legal practices must ensure that any processing of personal data for which they are responsible complies with the DPA. Failure to ensure compliance risks enforcement action, fines, prosecution and compensation claims or complaints from individuals.

The legal practice's policies and procedures must be relevant, workable and proportionate for the legal practice, taking into account its business model and how it operates to gain full support from everyone, whether manager/partner, owner or employee.

The legal practice's policies and procedures will need to cover:

- risk assessment (see **Chapter 2**);
- client inception (see **Chapter 3**);
- ongoing monitoring (see **Chapter 4**);
- data security (see **Chapter 5**);
- third parties (see **Chapter 6**);
- subject access requests (see **Chapter 7**);
- complaints handling (see **Chapter 8**);
- data retention/destruction (see **Chapter 9**);
- training (see **Chapter 10**);
- monitoring (see **Chapter 11**).

You should consider the following when drafting your policies and procedures:

- Differing types of data held.
- Where the data is held, who holds the data and how it is held.
- Who can access the data.
- Which third parties you use and what due diligence is undertaken on them.
- How accurate and up to date the data is.
- Arrangements for keeping data secure.
- Whether all devices will be encrypted.
- Whether external devices can be used, e.g. USB sticks in a secure way.
- Whether all PCs and laptops are 'locked down' so it is not possible to insert, e.g. a USB stick or a DVD.
- Whether employees can transfer data to their own devices/computers.
- How long you will hold the data for and how it will be destroyed safely.

In drafting the policies, you should also consider how employees will be affected, e.g. in relation to subject access requests and if the legal practice monitors and stores emails. Legal practices may consult Part 3 of the ICO's consolidated

Employment Practices Data Protection Code. The code gives guidance for businesses on monitoring or recording emails in the workplace.

The draft policy at **Annex 1A** covers data protection, confidentiality and information security in one policy. However, legal practices may prefer to have three separate policies, as envisaged by the relevant practice notes (as well as a separate business continuity policy).

Each legal practice will consider the best option for its business. The advantage of having one policy is that all the topics are covered in one place, reducing the risk that the topics are seen as separate and unconnected. Separate policies may result in a lack of clarity as to who is responsible for what issue.

On the other hand, practices may find it more confusing to cover all of the issues in one policy, particularly where a practice wishes to include more detail on, for example, information security issues.

If a practice has separate data protection, information security and confidentiality policies, it will be important to ensure that those policies are cross-referenced and ultimately that employees are clear as to their obligations and where to go for help.

1.7 Review/update of existing systems and procedures

Your systems and procedures need to be reviewed and kept up to date so they remain relevant and appropriate for your practice. They should be easy to use and sufficiently robust and proportionate, particularly in terms of clients. Systems will need to be cost-effective and practical.

When reviewing your systems and procedures, the following questions may be helpful:

- Have you had any recent confidentiality incidents; what happened and why?
- Have you had any subject access requests; were they complied with and in the timescale?
- How long do you keep files for?
- Do you tell clients how you will use their data?
- Do you use cookies (small files which are downloaded on to a device, e.g. a computer when a website is accessed and which allow that website to recognise that device)?
- Are you compliant with the Privacy and Electronic Communications (EC Directive) Regulations 2003 (SI 2003/2426) (PECR) in terms of your marketing?
- When did you last train your employees?

Marketing issues including the requirements about opt-ins and websites are considered in more detail in **Chapter 3**.

1.8 Training

Regular and effective training is critical so employees understand their obligations and raise queries or seek guidance at the earliest opportunity. **Chapter 10** provides further guidance on the relevant issues.

1.9 Monitoring

Failure to comply with the regulatory requirements leaves the legal practice open to regulatory and criminal sanctions. You need to monitor whether your systems are working effectively and take appropriate action if there is non-compliance (see **Chapter 11**).

1.10 Using the toolkit

The policy and procedure attached to this chapter should be completed after you have completed the risk identification matrix (**Annex 2B**) and risk mitigation form (**Annex 2D**) in **Chapter 2**.

Annex 1A

Data protection, confidentiality and information security policy

Purpose

This policy sets out how [*legal practice name*] complies with the Data Protection Act 1998 (DPA), confidentiality issues, information security and the SRA's regulatory requirements including outcome 7.5 and chapter 4 of the SRA Code of Conduct 2011.

Application

This policy applies to all managers and employees of [*legal practice name*], including those undertaking work through a consultancy arrangement, in a volunteer capacity, on a temporary basis, or through an agency. The term 'employees' is used to refer to managers and employees.

All employees must familiarise themselves, and comply with, this policy and related procedures. Failure to comply with this policy and the related procedures [will/may] result in disciplinary action because of the significant risks of fines, enforcement action, reputational consequences and disciplinary action.

Responsibilities

All employees are responsible for ensuring that all types of data are properly protected. Any issues or concerns about the DPA must be raised with the [DP officer/deputy DP officer/COLP/compliance team].

Relevant legislation

The following legislation must be complied with:

- Data Protection Act 1998 (DPA);
- Computer Misuse Act 1990;
- Regulation of Investigatory Powers Act 2000;
- Telecommunications (Lawful Business Practice) (Interception of Communications) Regulations 2000 (SI 2000/2699);
- Privacy and Electronic Communications (EC Directive) Regulations 2003 (SI 2003/2426);
- SRA Code of Conduct 2011.

Principles

The importance of keeping clients' affairs confidential, protecting personal and sensitive personal data and keeping information secure is fundamental. This policy is designed to cover all these areas so that all employees are clear about their obligations and how to protect data/ensure confidential information is kept confidential.

The DPA establishes a framework of rights and duties designed to protect personal data. The DPA requires that personal data is processed in compliance with the DPA and in accordance with the eight data protection principles. There are specific obligations particularly in relation to an individual's right to access data held about him or her.

Chapter 4 of the SRA Code of Conduct 2011 contains the requirements relating to the duty of confidentiality. While solicitors have a duty to keep clients' affairs confidential, they must also ensure that information belonging to employees, suppliers and third parties is kept confidential. Confidential information can only be released if the individual consents or if that duty is overridden by law, e.g. the money laundering legislation.

The seventh data protection principle requires [*legal practice name*] to have appropriate security to prevent personal data from being accidentally or deliberately compromised.

Employees are reminded that under the Computer Misuse Act 1990, there are three criminal offences:

s.1: Unauthorised access to computer material.
s.2: Unauthorised access with intent to commit or facilitate the commission of further offences.
s.3: Unauthorised modification of computer material.

Employees who are unsure as to whether they are able to access or modify material must contact [the DP officer/deputy DP officer/COLP/compliance officer] for guidance. Any commission of or attempt to commit a criminal offence by an employee will be dealt with in accordance with [*legal practice name*]'s disciplinary policy.

[As [*legal practice name*] monitors [and/or] stores the electronic communications of fee earners and other employees for business/security reasons, [*legal practice name*] must comply with the relevant provisions of the Regulatory and Investigatory Powers Act 2000 and the Telecommunications (Lawful Business Practice) (Interception of Communications) Regulations 2000 (SI 2000/2699). Further information is contained in the [Employee Handbook/the Employment policies].]

All employees must keep information about the clients and [*legal practice name*] secure at all times. If an employee is concerned that data and sensitive personal data or confidential information is at risk, he or she must immediately contact the [DP officer/deputy DP officer/COLP/compliance team].

Data protection

[*Legal practice name*] must keep certain information on its clients, employees and suppliers to carry out its day-to-day operations, to meet its objectives and to comply with legal obligations. The DPA applies to personal data and sensitive personal data but [*legal practice name*] must keep all client (and employee) information confidential and all information secure.

[*Legal practice name*] is committed to ensuring personal data is dealt with in compliance with the DPA. The aim of the DPA is to protect the rights of individuals (data subjects) about whom [*legal practice name*] holds 'personal data'.

The DPA imposes duties on those who decide how and why such data is processed (data controllers). The definition of 'processing' is obtaining, using, holding, amending, disclosing, destroying or deleting personal data.

[*Legal practice name*] is registered with the Information Commissioner as a data controller. The DP officer is [*name*]. [The deputy DP officer is [*name*]].

'Personal data' means data which relates to a living individual who can be identified from that data or from that data and other information which is in the possession of or likely to come into the possession of [*legal practice name*]. Examples are a person's name, address and date of birth but the definition also includes information which allows an individual to be identified, e.g. a unique reference number. The definition includes any expression of opinion about the individual and any indications of the intentions of the data controller or any other person in respect of the individual.

Personal data includes all data held electronically but also data held in a 'relevant filing system', i.e. non-automated records which are structured in a way which allows ready access to information about individuals.

All personal data must be processed in accordance with the eight data protection principles which require that data will:

- be obtained fairly and lawfully and not be processed unless certain conditions are met;
- be obtained for a specific and lawful purpose;
- be adequate, relevant but not excessive;
- be accurate and kept up to date;
- not be held longer than necessary;
- be processed in accordance with the rights of data subjects;
- be subject to appropriate security measures;
- not be transferred outside the European Economic Area (EEA).

[*Legal practice name*] must process personal data in accordance with one of the conditions for processing (usually consent) and fairly and lawfully.

Clients are provided with the necessary information about how their data will be processed in the client care letter/terms of business. If clients have any queries, employees must contact the [DP officer/deputy DP officer/COLP/compliance team] for advice.

Sensitive personal data

[*Legal practice name*] processes data about clients which will include sensitive personal data. The terms of business explain to clients how their data will be processed and seek explicit consent to the processing. If a client has a query about sensitive personal data, guidance should be sought from the DP officer.

All employees must ensure that they recognise sensitive personal data.

All employees must ensure that, wherever the data is held, i.e. on computer or in a relevant filing system (or a paper file), it is properly protected and held securely.

Sensitive personal data is personal data about:

(a) racial or ethnic origin;
(b) political opinions;
(c) religious or other beliefs of a similar nature;
(d) trade union membership;
(e) physical or mental health or condition;
(f) sexual life;
(g) the commission or alleged commission of any offence;
(h) any proceedings for any offence committed or alleged to have been committed, the disposal of such proceedings or the sentence of any court in such proceedings.

All employees will be trained on data protection issues and must attend the data protection training so that they understand what is meant by personal data and sensitive personal data and what their obligations are.

Employees

[*Legal practice name*] also processes data about prospective and current employees in accordance with [*legal practice name*]'s HR policies and the employment legislation as follows:

• Information on applicants for posts, including references.
• Employee information – contact details, bank account number, payroll information, supervision and appraisal notes.

All employees must comply with the same obligations in relation to employee data as they do in relation to client data.

Duty of confidentiality

The duty of confidentiality to clients is a fundamental duty for solicitors and their employees. Outcome 4.1 of the SRA Code of Conduct 2011 requires that the affairs of clients are kept confidential unless disclosure is required or permitted by law or the client consents.

Employees must tell a client all the information relevant to that retainer of which he or she has personal knowledge under outcome 4.2. Where the duty of confidentiality to one client conflicts with the duty of disclosure to another client, the duty of confidentiality takes precedence under outcome 4.3. Employees must ensure that they comply with [*legal practice name*]'s conflicts policy.

Employees must comply with outcome 4.4 and must not act for client A in a matter where A has an interest adverse to client B and B is a client for whom confidential information is held which is material to A in that matter. The only exception to that prohibition is where a legal practice is able to use an information barrier. [*Legal practice name*] [does/does not] use information barriers [as permitted by the relevant procedure].

[*Legal practice name*] has effective systems and controls which are set out in the policies and procedures to identify risks to client confidentiality and to mitigate those risks, as required by outcome 4.5. Employees must comply with [*legal practice name*]'s policies and procedures.

Employees must ensure conversations about client matters, which take place outside a secure environment, e.g. in the reception area, the lift and outside the office (especially with mobile phone conversations in public places, including trains) cannot be overheard.

Employees must not name clients or inform or confirm to a third party that [*legal practice name*] acts for someone unless that client has expressly given consent. This extends to enquiries from law enforcement as to whether [*legal practice name*] is acting for a particular individual which must be dealt with in accordance with the policy on responding to requests from law enforcement.

Employees must not answer any questions from the press or even confirm that [*legal practice name*] is acting for a particular client. Employees cannot provide an address (but can offer to pass on a letter to a client) and must refer all enquiries to the [DP officer/deputy DP officer/compliance team] or or the supervising partner.

When in court, employees must ensure that they do not discuss the client's matter in the hearing of the press or third parties, including the other parties to the case unless it is in the course of carrying out the client's instructions.

All employees must be aware of their duties under this policy and keep clients' affairs confidential except in the following situations:

- the client consents or asks that confidential information be provided;
- confidential information has to be provided by law.

All employees must comply with this policy and related procedures, attend training provided, raise any queries with the [DP officer/deputy DP officer/COLP/compliance team] and report any breaches or allegations or suspicions of breaches of confidentiality to the [DP officer/deputy DP officer/COLP/compliance team].

While the above provisions relate to clients, employees must ensure that they also keep information about other employees, third parties and suppliers confidential, as required by the law of confidence. The provisions apply equally to other employees, third parties and suppliers.

Personal conflicts

If employees have any personal knowledge of or any close connection to the client or others involved in any matter on which they are working, they must comply with [*legal practice name*]'s conflicts policy.

Information security

All files, laptops, smartphones and mobile phones must be kept with the employee at all times to minimise the risk of breaches of confidentiality and ensure that information is kept securely.

All electronic devices issued by the legal practice will be encrypted so that the risk of data loss is reduced. Employees must comply with [*legal practice name*]'s policy in relation to any confidential information which may be held on their personal devices.

Employees are not permitted to use USB sticks, or other mechanisms of transferring data, on electronic devices owned by [*legal practice name*] unless approval has been received from the [DP officer/deputy DP officer/IT/COLP].

When out of the office, files/papers must not be carried in a way which shows information that can identify the client (e.g. Mrs McGregor, 43 Acacia Avenue, Divorce). Files/papers must not be left in unlocked cars, and in no circumstances in cars overnight. If it is unavoidable, e.g. due to another appointment or court hearing, files/papers [may/must] be kept in the boot of a locked car.

All waste/unwanted letters and documents (including drafts and unwanted photocopies) must be disposed of securely [in the confidential waste/*other*].

Employees must not:

- install any software without authorisation;
- disclose their password to anyone else;
- use other people's log-in details;
- take equipment, data, information sources or software offsite unless they have written authority to do so;
- copy files from the network server into a personal directory without authority.

Employees must:

- log off when leaving their PC or workstation unattended;
- change their password, if it appears to have been found out/in accordance with [*legal practice name*]'s policy;

- ensure that no member of the public has access to the computer system;
- always ensure laptops and mobile devices are secured in unattended offices;
- ensure data is transferred between laptops/mobile devices and the main system as soon as possible to preserve its integrity and in accordance with [*legal practice name*]'s policy;
- keep master copies of important data on the network server and not on a PC's local C drive or USB sticks. Data will not be backed up unless it is on the network server and so it is at risk;
- ask for advice from [IT/DP officer/deputy DP officer], if it is necessary to store, transmit or handle large quantities of data, e.g. DVDs or images.

If there is any loss of data or risk of loss, employees must immediately contact the [DP officer/deputy DP officer/COLP/compliance team] who will advise what to do next.

Subject access requests (SARs)

The DPA gives individuals the right to access personal data held about them on computer and in relevant filing systems. Any person wishing to exercise this right should apply in writing to the [DP officer/deputy officer/COLP/compliance team]. The terms of business provide details of how to make a SAR.

If a request is made quoting the DPA or if an individual makes a subject access request, that must be referred to the [DP officer/deputy officer/COLP/compliance team] immediately. Clients may also ask for details of information held about them without mentioning the word 'data' or the data protection legislation; all such requests must be forwarded immediately to the [DP officer/deputy officer/COLP/compliance team] as that request may still be a SAR.

There are strict timescales for compliance with a SAR and failure to comply can result in a significant fine from the ICO. Employees must comply with [*legal practice name*]'s procedure for dealing with SARs.

Accuracy of data

Employees must ensure that data is as accurate as possible; if data is or appears to be inaccurate, misleading or not up to date, employees must take reasonable steps to amend/update the information as soon as possible. Data only needs to be kept up to date where necessary and employees should seek guidance if they are not sure whether the data needs to be updated. Clients have the right to prevent processing of their personal data in some circumstances and the right to correct, rectify, block or erase information regarded as wrong. Any concerns must be discussed with the [DP officer/deputy DP officer/COLP/compliance team].

Retention and destruction of data

Personal data must be retained or disposed of securely in accordance with [*legal practice name*]'s data retention and destruction policy.

Data controllers/processors

Personal data must not be disclosed to another party unless they are a data controller or a data processor (as defined in this policy), it is for the purposes of the case. The client must always be advised to whom the data will be disclosed and why.

Before sending data to a data controller or a data processor, the employee must ensure that proper contractual arrangements are in place to protect the data. Alternatively the employee must contact the [DP officer/deputy DP officer/COLP/ compliance team] to determine whether there is already a contractual arrangement or what further steps need to be taken. [*Legal practice name*] must ensure that the data controller or data processor understands the basis on which they will hold the data, when they will return it, what the security arrangements are and what will happen if there is any data loss.

The [DP officer/deputy DP officer/COLP/compliance team] is responsible for ensuring that appropriate due diligence is undertaken and that [*legal practice name*] is registered with the ICO. The [DP officer/deputy DP officer/COLP/compliance team] will record the details of the data controller or data processor on the data controller/data processor log. If an employee has any queries about the way in which a data controller or data processor is dealing with data, he or she must contact the [DP officer/deputy DP officer/COLP/compliance team].

Breaches of policy

Breaches of this policy may require disclosure to the SRA, which may result in disciplinary action, given the obligations under chapter 10 of the SRA Code of Conduct 2011. A report may also need to be made to the ICO under [*legal practice name*]'s policy on reporting to the ICO.

Further advice

If there are concerns regarding a client or a retainer and potential breaches of confidentiality, employees must contact the [DP officer/deputy DP officer/COLP/ compliance team] immediately for advice.

Definitions

Personal data – data which relates to a living individual who can be identified from that data, or from that data and other information which is in the possession of, or is likely to come into the possession of, the data controller, and includes any expression of opinion about the individual and any indication of the intentions of the data controller or any other person in respect of the individual.

Data subject means a living individual who is the subject of personal data.

Data controller means a person (usually an organisation) who (alone or jointly or in common with other persons) determines the purposes for which and the manner in which any personal data is, or is to be, processed. However, two or more persons (usually organisations) can be joint data controllers where they act together to decide the purpose and manner of any data processing. The term 'in common' applies where two or more persons share a pool of personal data that they process independently of each other.

Data processor – in relation to personal data, means any person (other than an employee of the data controller) who processes the data on behalf of the data controller.

Related policies and procedures

The following policies and procedures must be considered when complying with this policy:

- Disciplinary policy
- Subject access request procedure
- Responding to requests from third parties policy
- Reporting to the ICO policy
- Data retention and destruction procedure
- Ongoing monitoring procedure
- Social media policy
- Data loss policy
- DPA complaints policy
- Training procedure.

Glossary

COLP	compliance officer for legal practice
DPA	Data Protection Act 1998
DP officer	data protection officer
ICO	Information Commissioner's Office
SAR	subject access request
SRA	Solicitors Regulation Authority

Date of effect/date of review

This policy shall come into effect on [*date*] and will be reviewed annually.

Annex 1B

Procedure for appointing the data protection officer

Purpose

This procedure sets out how [*legal practice name*] will appoint its DP officer and any deputies in accordance with its DP obligations. It sets out the main responsibilities of the DP officer and any deputies and how they will report to the [management board/partnership/*other*] on the discharge of those duties.

Who is eligible to be the DP officer or deputy DP officer?

The DP officer (and any deputy) shall be of sufficient seniority to:

- have access to all client and employee files, accounting records and other information;
- make decisions on complex data protection queries;
- make decisions on how to deal with subject access requests;
- deal with data protection breaches/data loss, in liaison with the COLP;
- make decisions on whether to make a report to the ICO.

For [*legal practice name*] the DP officer may be [*e.g. a senior partner, a managing partner, a partner, a director, an associate director, the chief operating officer*].

For [*legal practice name*] the deputy DP officer may be [*e.g. a senior partner, a managing partner, a partner, a director, an associate director, the chief operating officer*].

How will the DP officer and any deputies be appointed?

The DP officer will be appointed by the [management board/partnership/*other*] and the appointment will be recorded. The DP officer must consent to the appointment.

[*Number*] deputy DP officer[s] will also be appointed by the [management board/partnership/*other*] and the appointment will be recorded. The deputy DP officer[s] must consent to the appointment.

The roles of DP officer and deputy DP officer will be subject to reappointment every [*number*] years.

The appointments will be recorded by the [management board/partnership/*other*] and the acceptance of the appointment will be endorsed by the DP officer or deputy DP officer[s].

What are the DP officer's responsibilities?

In discussion with the [management board/partnership/*other*], the DP officer is responsible for:

- setting the policies and procedures for compliance with [*legal practice name*]'s DP obligations;
- conducting the risk assessment for [*legal practice name*];
- establishing the DP training programme for [*legal practice name*].

The DP officer is responsible for:

- registering with the ICO, keeping the registration up to date and renewing it annually;
- ensuring he or she [and the compliance team] remains up to date on data protection/information security developments and relevant case law;
- providing advice on DP queries;
- ensuring that subject access requests and other legitimate DPA requests are handled in accordance with the appropriate timescales/in a timely manner;
- advising on potential data protection incidents in liaison with the COLP;
- deciding whether to make a report to the ICO and liaising with the ICO;
- liaising with managers/partners and employees on the conduct of retainers where there are DP concerns;
- assisting HR with employee-related DP queries;
- liaising with data controllers, data processors or third parties;
- regularly auditing the practice's use of personal data and checking to ensure compliance;
- amending/updating the data protection policies and procedures and ensuring that all employees and partners are aware of, understand and comply with the policies and procedures;
- providing advice on the data protection implications of new products/services and new information security/IT systems and procedures;
- advising the [management board/partnership/*other*] on the level of resources required for appropriate DP compliance;
- reporting [annually/every six months] to the [management board/partnership/*other*] on [*legal practice name*]'s compliance with DP obligations.

What are the deputy DP officer's responsibilities?

The deputy DP officer will assist the DP officer with the discharge of his or her functions and will take on the full role of DP officer in the DP officer's absence, including dealing with subject access requests.

[Each deputy DP officer will specifically provide advice and assistance on DP compliance to managers/partners and employees in his or her designated [office/practice area].]

Related policy

Data protection policy and policies/procedures referred to in that policy

Glossary

COLP	compliance officer for legal practice
DP	data protection
DP officer	data protection officer
HR	human resources
ICO	Information Commissioner's Office

Date of effect/date of review

This procedure shall come into effect on [*date*]. This procedure shall be reviewed annually.

Annex 1C
Record of appointment of the data protection officer

The [management board/partnership/*other*] of [*legal practice name*] at its meeting of [*date*] appointed the following individual[s] to discharge the role[s] of data protection officer [for the period of [*years*]/until further notice].

Name of [senior partner/managing partner/CEO/*other*]:	
Signature:	
Date:	

Data protection officer

Name:	
Role in [*legal practice name*]:	
Signature accepting appointment:	

[*Delete the following if necessary:*]

Deputy data protection officer

Name:	
Role in [*legal practice name*]:	
[Office or practice area of responsibility:]	
Signature accepting appointment:	

Deputy data protection officer

Name:	
Role in [*legal practice name*]:	
[Office or practice area of responsibility:]	
Signature accepting appointment:	

Annex 1D

Data protection principles – Data Protection Act 1998, Schedule 1

1. Personal data shall be processed fairly and lawfully and, in particular, shall not be processed unless–

    (a) at least one of the conditions in Schedule 2 is met, and
    (b) in the case of sensitive personal data, at least one of the conditions in Schedule 3 is also met.

2. Personal data shall be obtained only for one or more specified and lawful purposes, and shall not be further processed in any manner incompatible with that purpose or those purposes.
3. Personal data shall be adequate, relevant and not excessive in relation to the purpose or purposes for which they are processed.
4. Personal data shall be accurate and, where necessary, kept up to date.
5. Personal data processed for any purpose or purposes shall not be kept for longer than is necessary for that purpose or those purposes.
6. Personal data shall be processed in accordance with the rights of data subjects under this Act.
7. Appropriate technical and organisational measures shall be taken against unauthorised or unlawful processing of personal data and against accidental loss or destruction of, or damage to, personal data.
8. Personal data shall not be transferred to a country or territory outside the European Economic Area unless that country or territory ensures an adequate level of protection for the rights and freedoms of data subjects in relation to the processing of personal data.

2 Managing the risk to the legal practice

2.1 Overview

Risk management is a concept with which legal practices should now be familiar and they should have systems in place to identify, monitor and manage risk, as required by chapter 7 of the SRA Code, in particular outcome 7.3. In addition, outcome 7.5 requires legal practices to comply with legislation applicable to the business including anti-money laundering and data protection legislation.

The Solicitors Regulation Authority (SRA) is a risk-based regulator and it states that risk is central to everything it does. The SRA's Regulatory Risk Framework, the Risk Index and the Risk Outlook (published in July 2013) and the November 2013 and March 2014 Updates including guidance on cloud computing, provide practices with a considerable amount of information to help them to identify the risks for their practices.

Before setting up new procedures or reviewing existing procedures, the DP officer, COLP and senior management need to identify and document the DP, confidentiality and information security risks which specifically apply to the legal practice. Once identified, these can be added to the risk register.

You need to assess whether you are managing those risks, through your systems and controls, including your policies and procedures. Are your policies and procedures up to date? Have you trained all your employees on the DP legislation relevant to their areas and on what they need to do?

This assessment should enable you to identify what changes, if any are required. If changes are required, a legal practice should update its compliance plan (see rule 8 of the SRA Authorisation Rules for Legal Services Bodies and Licensable Bodies 2011).

Both the risk register and the compliance plan should be reviewed regularly by the COLP and the DP officer to identify any new or potential risks, e.g. strategic changes to the legal practice such as merging with another legal practice, taking on a new area of work or branching out into a new jurisdiction as well as any changes to current risks. This review is likely to form part of the DP officer's annual report to management (see **Chapter 11**).

2.2 Using the toolkit

Assessing the data protection risks for your practice may seem challenging but the starting point is to consider what data you hold, why you hold it, where it is held (and how securely), for whom you hold it and whether the data is held with any data controllers or data processors, e.g. expert witnesses.

The risk assessment procedure at **Annex 2A** will help the legal practice determine the issues relevant to its practice. The key 'assessors' will be the COLP and the DP officer who will need to involve the right people in the practice, e.g. those responsible for information security to ensure that all relevant issues are identified.

Your assessment should cover what your key assets are, both tangible (buildings, stock and money) and intangible (client data, your intellectual property) and assess how secure they are (in terms of both internal and external threats). Understanding what data the practice holds will be a crucial part of the risk assessment, so that appropriate steps can be taken in terms of both processing and protection of the data. Legal practices may wish to use a checklist so that the right information is obtained in each matter/practice area and so that unnecessary data is not obtained.

The value of an asset may not be immediately apparent, for example, the loss of data could be used to facilitate a fraud against your practice, client or a third party, such as identity theft.

The risk identification matrix (**Annex 2B**) sets out common DP risk factors faced by legal practices and indicates general risk categories. The aim of the matrix is to provide a starting point to enable legal practices to assess their own risks. Equally, legal practices may take a different view of the risks. While a corporate client may be low risk, a legal practice advising a corporate client on an employment case is likely to see that as medium risk because of the need to protect the employee's personal data. While advising clients on their financial affairs will be medium risk, advising a financial institution on the Financial Services and Markets Act 2000 is likely to be low risk as it is less likely to involve personal data.

The DP officer, the COLP, IT and senior management should discuss which of the risk factors are present in the legal practice and simply circle them on the form. You may need to add areas of practice, client types or jurisdictions. If certain types of clients only instruct one area of practice, then that should be noted. If the suggested risk category for a particular factor is not appropriate, you should document the reason why. The matrix can be amended to reflect the risks present in your legal practice.

The purpose of the risk identification matrix is to ensure that the legal practice has a shared understanding of the DP risks faced by the practice and can take steps to mitigate those risks.

The sensitive personal data list (**Annex 2C**) is designed to be an easy reminder for employees so that they keep alert to the need to take greater care with such data. This list, along with the completed risk identification matrix, should be available to employees, e.g. on the legal practice's intranet.

The risk mitigation form (**Annex 2D**) should be completed by the DP officer and senior management to set out the high-level approach and resourcing decisions which are being taken to enable compliance. These decisions will then determine the options selected by the DP officer in adapting the remaining procedures and forms in the toolkit to the specific requirements of the legal practice.

Annex 2A
Data protection and information security risk assessment procedure

Purpose

This procedure sets out how [*legal practice name*] will assess the risks associated with data protection, confidentiality and information security for the practice.

Application

This procedure applies to senior management, the DP officer and the COLP.

Initial risk assessment

The [board/partnership/management team/*other*], DP officer and COLP will identify, assess and record the data protection and information security risks applicable to [*legal practice name*] using [the risk identification matrix/*other*].

Taking into account the risks identified, the [board/partnership/management team/*other*], DP officer and COLP will complete the risk mitigation form, setting out how the legal practice will meet its regulatory and legal obligations.

The [COLP/DP officer] will ensure that this information is added to the risk register and compliance plan for [*legal practice name*].

Ongoing risk assessment

The [board/partnership/management team/*other*], DP officer and COLP will review the risk profile of the legal practice whenever [*legal practice name*] considers any significant change to its business model, including:

- merging with or taking over another legal practice;
- entering into a referral arrangement or best-friend relationship with another organisation;
- introduction of new information security/IT systems or significant changes to existing systems;
- introduction of new services or products;
- opening a new office;
- undertaking a new area of practice;
- seeking clients from a new jurisdiction or a new domestic market with links to a foreign jurisdiction.

The DP officer will review the risk profile of [*legal practice name*] during the preparation of the DP officer's annual report to management.

Communication to employees

The completed risk profile of [*legal practice name*] and the sensitive personal data list will be made available to all employees of [*legal practice name*] through the [intranet/*other*].

Related policy

Data protection, information security and confidentiality policy

Glossary

COLP   compliance officer for legal practice
DP officer   data protection officer

Date of effect/date of review

This procedure shall come into effect on [*date*]. This procedure shall be reviewed annually.

Annex 2B
Risk identification matrix

Legal practice features

Feature	Risk issues to consider
Single office	• Whether you need to have only one deputy DP officer to cover absences • Whether simpler systems are appropriate, as consistency should be easier to monitor • Whether to make use of external training support, e.g. for access to sufficient case studies to help employees appreciate emerging or unusual risks
Multiple domestic offices	• Having deputy DP officers for each office to ensure sufficient expertise is available to employees • The need to have more formalised systems to ensure consistency of approach • How management will have an effective overview of compliance across all offices • How you will deploy training effectively and efficiently
Multiple overseas offices	• Different DP, confidentiality and information security obligations in each jurisdiction and how you will transfer clients between jurisdictions • Having deputy DP officers for each office or jurisdiction to ensure sufficient expertise is available to employees • The need to have more formalised systems to ensure consistency • How management will have an effective overview of compliance across all offices • How you will deploy training effectively and efficiently, taking account of different jurisdictional challenges
Limited central support function	• Who will assess the data protection/information security risks for the practice and the need to ensure those employees receive appropriate training on DP and information security issues • How you will ensure sufficient expertise is available to all employees • The need to have more extensive monitoring options for compliance
Full central support function	• Where data protection/information security risks are managed by a central team, the need to ensure that employees see and understand the risks for ongoing monitoring purposes, having received appropriate training • The central team need to be trained in detail on the information security and data protection procedures and be able to provide advice to the practice areas • The central team may be able to assist with monitoring compliance and identifying emerging risks and lessons learnt
Paper-based filing system	• Where personal data will be stored and kept up to date so that it can be accessed by fee earners and the DP officer • How monitoring of compliance with DP obligations will be undertaken • How the practice will ensure that personal data is properly protected • Who will be responsible for information security

Integrated electronic case management and record-keeping system	• How personal data will be recorded on the system • Who will be responsible for keeping the data up to date and accurate • Who will be responsible for information security • Which personal data will be accessible to different parts of the legal practice • How the practice will ensure that personal data is properly protected • How relevant reports can be generated to assist with monitoring compliance of data protection obligations
High use of paralegals and junior employees	• The need to have more formalised procedures and more frequent monitoring • The need to enhance the capacity of the DP officer to answer queries on a more regular basis
High use of qualified and senior employees	• Whether you may be able to provide greater flexibility in procedures and give greater discretion to managers/partners • The need for the DP officer to be available as required
Third parties	• Will the practice share data with third parties, if so who • Will data be received from third parties • How the practice will ensure that the third parties properly protect the data • Who will be responsible for monitoring the third parties and their compliance

General risk categories for areas of practice, jurisdiction and clients

High risk	Medium risk	Low risk

• Personal injury clients (including clinical negligence)
• Court of Protection clients
• Criminal clients
• Employment clients
• Foreign clients (outside the EU)
• Cases involving sensitive personal data of clients [see **Annex 2C**]
  – Racial or ethnic origin
  – Sexual life
  – Physical or mental health or condition
  – Religious or similar beliefs
  – Trade union membership
  – Political opinions
• Personal injury litigation
• Mental health and incapacity law
• Criminal law
• Employment law
• Trusts and probate, including acting as an attorney
• Court of Protection work
	• Family and matrimonial clients
	• Conveyancing clients
	• Debt recovery clients
	• Foreign clients (within the EU)
	• Trust and probate clients (unless sensitive personal data is held)
	• Will writing clients (unless sensitive personal data is held)
	• Professional negligence clients (except clinical negligence)
	• Financial services clients
	• Cases involving personal data of private clients
	  – Name, address, date of birth
	  – Financial records
	  – Opinions about clients
	• Matrimonial and family law
	• Children law
	• Property law, both commercial and residential
	• Landlord and tenant law
	• Debt recovery and mortgage repossession
	• Acting as a Court of Protection deputy
	• Will writing
	• Professional negligence litigation
	• Insolvency, bankruptcy and receivership
	• Tax law
	• Financial services advice
		• Planning clients
		• Corporate clients
		• Charities
		• Financial Conduct Authority regulated businesses
		• Local authorities or domestic government departments
		• Planning law
		• Corporate law, including company creation, management and acquisition
		• Corporate finance
		• Commercial litigation
		• Charity law
		• Financial services law
		• Government-funded work
		• Environmental, energy and natural resources law
		• Construction law
		• Intellectual property law
		• Shipping and aviation law

Annex 2C

Sensitive personal data

Under the first data protection principle, personal data shall not be processed unless at least one of the conditions in Schedule 2 to the Data Protection Act 1998 (DPA) is met and in the case of sensitive personal data, at least one of the conditions in Schedule 3 is met.

In addition, legal practices need to ensure that the level of security is appropriate to the nature of the data to be protected (see the seventh data protection principle and para.9(b) of Part II of Schedule 1 to the DPA) because of the risk that the data could be used in a discriminatory way. Employees must ensure that they comply with the policies and procedures of the legal practice when handling sensitive personal data and if they are unsure of their responsibilities, seek guidance from the DP officer.

Sensitive personal data means personal data consisting of information as to:

(a) racial or ethnic origin of the data subject;
(b) his political opinions;
(c) his religious or other beliefs of a similar nature;
(d) whether he is a member of a trade union;
(e) his physical or mental health or condition;
(f) his sexual life;
(g) the commission or alleged commission by him of any offence;
(h) any proceedings for any offence committed or alleged to have been committed by him, the disposal of such proceedings or the sentence of any court in such proceedings.

When processing sensitive personal data, all employees must ensure that the right data is sent to the right client or the right third party and consider extra security, for example, by anonymising it, password protecting the data or sending it more securely.

Annex 2D
Risk mitigation form

Key risk areas
List the practice areas which are high risk or involve high-risk clients or jurisdictions:
Outline the legal practice's risk exposure to loss of personal data:
Outline the legal practice's risk exposure to loss of sensitive personal data:

Discharging the DP officer function
Outline the seniority of the DP officer, to whom he or she will report and the relevant support structures in place, including, where relevant, deputies and compliance team:
Outline who will prepare the DP and information security procedures and approve amendments:
Outline who will ensure information security measures are suitably robust and compliant with the DP legislation:
Outline how the DP officer will be supported on complex issues of data protection law:
Outline how decisions will be made to report data loss to the client:
Outline how decisions will be made to report severe data loss to the ICO and the SRA:

Personal data
List the clients and practice areas where sensitive personal data will be held:
List the types of sensitive personal data held and the practice area:
Outline how data is held: •   [centrally/on individual files] •   [paper based/electronically]
How are documents containing sensitive personal data kept secure?

Ensuring compliance
Outline who will be given training:
Outline how compliance will be monitored: • [internal audit team/external audits]

PART 2
Client interface

This section of the toolkit covers how the legal practice will ensure compliance with its data protection obligations.

3 Client inception

3.1 What issues should you consider?

When taking on clients, a legal practice will have to obtain detailed information about the clients and their instructions, in order to provide legal services. However, legal practices should ensure that data protection issues are carefully considered from the start of the retainer so that data is properly processed in compliance with the legislation. Failure to do so is likely to result in significant fines from the ICO and disciplinary action from the SRA.

The key issues to consider at client inception are:

- What data will you ask for and why?
- How is the data obtained?
- How will you process the data fairly and lawfully?
- What consent will you seek from the client?
- What information do you give to the client?
- What will you do with that data; will you share it with data controllers or data processors?
- Will you need to send the data overseas?
- How will you store the data securely?
- What will you do at the end of the case/matter?

It is important to consider not only what personal data you obtain but also how you obtain it:

- Is it obtained directly from the client or from a referrer or via the web?
- Is it clear what will happen to the personal data?
- Is it clear how the personal data will be used?

If the person, from whom the data is received, is deceived or misled as to the purpose or purposes for which the data is to be processed, that is likely to mean that the data has not been processed fairly; reference is made to DPA, Sched.1, Part II, para.1(1). If the client provides information to the insurer about the car accident, does the client know it will be provided to your legal practice to pursue a personal injury (PI) claim? Ensuring that there is transparency and clarity about the way in which the data is obtained and how it will be processed should minimise the risk that anyone is deceived or misled.

Legal practices should also consider how to process personal data about other individuals, e.g. opponents and employees in accordance with the data protection requirements.

Another challenge is that of client enquiries which do not proceed either because the instructions are not accepted or because the client decides to go elsewhere. Personal data will be obtained in such circumstances, although the amount of data will vary on a case-by-case basis. In some cases, it will simply be name and address but in other cases confidential information about the nature of the case will be obtained. Legal practices will consider how much information to retain, bearing in mind the conduct issues particularly in relation to conflict and confidentiality.

3.2 What data will you ask for and why?

In deciding what data to obtain from clients (and potential clients), legal practices should ensure:

- it is clear why data is being obtained and that it is obtained only for one or more specified and lawful purposes (second principle);
- that personal data is adequate, relevant and not excessive in relation to the purpose or purposes for which the data is processed (third principle);
- data is accurate and where necessary kept up to date (fourth principle);
- data is kept for no longer than necessary (fifth principle).

Legal practices and their employees need to understand why they are obtaining personal data, whether it is sensitive personal data and what the data will be used for, i.e. whether they have legitimate grounds for collecting and using that data. An example is the collection of client due diligence (CDD) information in a conveyancing matter to comply with the Money Laundering Regulations 2007 (SI 2007/2157) or obtaining medical records to progress a PI case.

A checklist or fact find for each practice area may help to ensure that employees only obtain the data necessary to provide the legal services. This is also good business practice as it will ensure that the right information has been obtained to progress the matter.

Legal practices should ensure they know what data is held so that the data can be kept up to date, where necessary, secure and accurate:

- If the client advises that he or she has moved house, what systems are there to ensure that records are updated accurately?
- What happens if there is an error in transposition, e.g. a date of birth?
- Will the practice accept a telephone call or is confirmation in writing required? (Changing an address on the basis of a telephone call leaves you open to fraud.)
- What happens if there appears to be a mistake/inaccuracy? How will the information be checked or will it be ignored?
- Clients may challenge the accuracy of medical opinions but if the records accurately reflect the diagnosis at the time, the record is not inaccurate.

Having clarity as to what data is held will also help legal practices to determine for how long the data will be held. It is likely that the data will need to be held for the duration of the retainer but how long does it need to be held for once the retainer is completed? **Chapter 9** covers data retention and destruction.

Legal practices need to be transparent about the way in which the data will be processed and give individuals appropriate privacy notices (or terms of business) (see **3.4**) so they are clear about what data is required and why, what the practice will do with it, with whom it will be shared, how it will be held and for how long it will be held. This also reduces the risk of complaints or criticism at a later stage.

Legal practices also need to consider what data they may receive from data controllers or third parties and what data they will share with data processors and why, e.g. counsel or expert witnesses as well as how they will handle and protect the data (see **Chapter 6**) and what contractual arrangements they will have in place.

3.3 How will you process the data fairly and lawfully?

There are two elements to the first data protection principle:

* Process the personal data fairly and lawfully.
* Meet at least one of the conditions in DPA, Sched.2 and in the case of sensitive personal data at least one of the conditions in DPA, Sched.3.

3.3.1 Fair and lawful processing

The reason for obtaining the data is to provide legal services and provided that excessive data is not collected, legal practices should not find it difficult to meet the fair and lawful processing requirement. Clients will need to be provided with a clear privacy notice (e.g. in the terms of business) so that they understand what the data will be used for, how it will be used and with whom it will be shared. Although the ICO says there is no point in telling people the obvious if it is clear what the information will be used for, legal practices will need to assess whether it is, in fact, obvious to the client and provide the client with sufficient information.

Legal practices should be aware that they must avoid unjustified adverse effects on the individuals concerned but in any event, outcome 1.1 of the SRA Code requires legal practices to treat clients fairly.

Legal practices will comply with the 'lawful' element by ensuring that they comply with the law and do not, e.g. infringe copyright or breach the Human Rights Act 1998.

3.3.2 Conditions for processing

Legal practices must meet one of the conditions for processing personal data in DPA, Sched.2 and in the case of sensitive personal data, one of the conditions in DPA, Sched.3. In most cases, a legal practice should be able to obtain the client's consent to processing by explaining clearly what personal data will be obtained and why at the start of the retainer. If the terms of business are signed by the client, that should be sufficient to demonstrate both the Sched.2 condition and, where applicable, the explicit consent condition for sensitive personal data. The full list of the Sched.2 and Sched.3 conditions is at **Annex 3C**.

It is important to consider whether you are likely to use or disclose personal data for a new purpose. For example, if the information is obtained in order to pursue litigation, the information should not be used for marketing purposes without consent. Most legal practices will include provisions about marketing within the terms of business (see **Annex 3A**).

3.4 What information will be given to the client?

Most legal practices will include a privacy notice within the terms of business although other options will be a notice on the website or a pre-recorded message at the start of a telephone call.

A privacy notice should tell the client who you are, what you intend to do with the data and with whom it will be shared. It should be in simple language, clear font and style and include a clear explanation as to why the data is required. In addition, the client should have a clear opportunity to agree to marketing or to opt out of marketing, see **3.9**. There are specific rules for marketing by email, telephone, fax, text or other forms of electronic messages contained in the Privacy and Electronic Communications (EC Directive) Regulations 2003 (SI 2003/2426) (PECR).

Legal practices should ensure that employees are familiar with the ways in which data may be processed, including the marketing provisions, so they consider the position of individual clients and are able to answer their queries.

3.5 What will you do with that data?

In order to provide legal services, legal practices will use the personal data received in a variety of ways. The data will be used, for example, to issue proceedings, seek expert advice from barristers or medical experts, or to give to insurers or other solicitors, e.g. to progress a claim.

During initial discussions with the client, the fee earner should make it clear what will happen with the personal data, e.g. medical records will be sent to medical experts to review and who will have to keep the data secure. **Chapter 6** sets out the issues to be considered in more detail.

3.6 Will you need to send the data overseas?

Legal practices will need to consider whether the data needs to be sent overseas, for example, in relation to multi-jurisdiction litigation. Under the eighth data protection principle, personal data shall not be transferred to a country or territory outside the EEA unless that country or territory ensures an adequate level of protection.

There are no restrictions on the transfer of personal data to the EEA countries and the European Commission has decided that certain other countries have an adequate level of protection for personal data. Those countries are Andorra, Argentina, Canada, Faroe Islands, Guernsey, Isle of Man, Israel, Jersey, New Zealand, Switzerland and Uruguay. The up-to-date list of such countries can be accessed at **http://ec.europa.eu/justice/data-protection/document/international-transfers/adequacy/index_en.htm.**

The USA is not included in the European Commission list but it is considered that personal data sent to the USA under the 'Safe Harbor' scheme is adequately protected. It is important to note that the US company must sign up to the 'Safe Harbor' arrangement; by doing so it agrees to follow seven principles of information handling and be held responsible for keeping to those principles by the Federal Trade Commission or other oversight schemes. Certain companies cannot sign up to 'Safe Harbor' but the companies which are signed up to 'Safe Harbor' can be accessed at **http://export.gov/safeharbor**.

If the data protection law in a country has not been approved as adequate, personal data can still be sent to that country if:

- the adequacy of the protection has been assessed by a legal practice;
- contracts are used including the European Commission approved model contractual clauses;
- the Binding Corporate Rules are approved by the Information Commissioner; or
- the legal practice relies on exceptions from the rule.

Further guidance on these points can be found in the ICO's Guide to Data Protection at chapter B8.

Personal data can also be transferred overseas if you have the client's consent which should be given clearly and freely and may later be withdrawn by the individual. (This provision does not apply to corporate clients.) If the reason for the transfer is to enable litigation to take place in another jurisdiction, the client is likely to give informed consent.

3.7 How will you store the data?

Legal practices should consider carefully how and where the data will be stored and who will be able to access it. Data will tend to be stored electronically and therefore the computer security will need to be appropriate to the size and use of the practice's systems. Specialist information security advice may be required as this is a complex technical area.

However, physical security is also relevant, not only in terms of protection of the premises but also as regards how you control access to premises, supervise visitors, dispose of paper waste and keep portable equipment secure. **Chapter 5** provides further assistance and **Annex 5B** sets out a range of security measures to consider.

If all employees in the legal practice are able to access all personal data, there will need to be robust security systems to protect that data. It may be more prudent to restrict access to sensitive personal data to those working on the case or within that department.

The security must be appropriate to the business needs but, for example, if there are employees working from home, there should be measures in place to ensure this does not compromise security; reference is made to the ICO's guidance 'Bring your own device (BYOD)'.

Legal practices should ensure there is a regular review of how data is stored, good liaison between the DP officer and the COLP (as well as IT) and ongoing monitoring of the risks so that improvements can be made to the systems and controls. The Law Society's *Lexcel Information Management Toolkit* (2nd edition, Law Society, 2013) will be helpful.

3.8 What will you do at the end of the case/matter?

Legal practices will need to consider what systems there are to deal with the data at the end of the matter, how the data will be retrieved from or destroyed by data processors, e.g. expert witnesses and how/when the data will be archived and ultimately destroyed.

Chapter 9 considers data retention and destruction issues in more detail.

Chapter 6 covers the issues in relation to data controllers/processors. Dealing with the personal data held by data controllers/processors at the end of the matter is arguably one of the greatest data protection challenges.

Legal practices will also consider how much information to retain on potential clients. Issues to consider include receipt/retention of confidential information and entering basic information into the case management system for conflict checking purposes.

3.9 Marketing issues

Legal practices must ensure that their systems and controls take account of the data protection issues in relation to marketing. Ensuring that those involved in business development/marketing are familiar with the data protection requirements is critical given the reputational consequences of non-compliance.

The main areas to consider are as follows:

- Cookies
- Direct marketing and opt in/opt out
- Publicising the names of clients
- Social media.

3.9.1 Cookies

Legal practices should already be aware of the regulations in PECR regarding cookies. The legislation was changed in May 2011 and under reg.6, those setting cookies must tell clients that the cookies are there, explain what the cookies are doing, and obtain clients' consent to store a cookie on their device. Since 2003 anyone using cookies has been required to provide clear information about those cookies. The requirements are such that those designing the website need to be familiar with the ICO's guidance on the rules on the use of cookies (**http://ico.org. uk/for_organisations/privacy_and_electronic_communications/the_guide/cookies**).

3.9.2 Direct marketing

Obtaining and retaining clients is key to the success of a legal practice but those involved in business development/marketing need to be familiar with the provisions of chapter 8 of the SRA Code as well as the legislation relating to marketing (see **Annex 3D**).

PECR apply to telephone calls, faxes, emails, text messages and other forms of electronic messages (e.g. via social networking sites).

Legal practices need to be familiar with the requirements, particularly in relation to the need for specific consent for recorded calls and faxes and specific consent or soft opt-in for emails and texts.

Soft opt-in is where the client is a previous client, the marketing relates to your own similar product and the client has had a chance to opt out. If a legal practice is seeking to make use of the soft opt-in in relation to texts and emails then an initial opportunity to refuse may not be sufficient on the grounds that the soft opt-in requires that the legal practice (amongst other requirements) 'gave the person a simple opportunity to refuse or opt out of the marketing, *both when first collecting the details and in every message after that*' [emphasis added] (see the ICO guidance on direct marketing, p.29, available at **http://ico.org.uk/for_organisations/ guidance_index/~/media/documents/library/Privacy_and_electronic/Practical_ application/direct-marketing-guidance.pdf**).

Legal practices may include a provision in the terms of business letter (**Annex 3A**) to give all clients the opportunity to refuse to receive direct marketing correspondence or contact.

Under outcome 8.3 of the SRA Code, a legal practice must not make unsolicited approaches in person or by telephone to members of the public, although unsolicited visits or telephone calls to a client or former client are permitted.

The ICO's direct marketing checklist may be helpful in determining the legal practice's approach to direct marketing and the need for consent. This is available at **http://ico.org.uk/~/media/documents/library/Privacy_and_electronic/Practical_ application/direct-marketing-checklist.pdf**.

3.9.3 Publicising the names of clients

If a legal practice wishes to publicise the name of the client, e.g. on a website or in a press release, it will need to seek the client's consent, after explaining the implications.

Legal practices should ensure either that consent is obtained from the client before information about the client's case is placed on the website or that the details are sufficiently anonymised so that the client cannot be identified. There may be occasions if the case is sufficiently unusual, when, despite the anonymisation, the identity of the client can still be ascertained.

Employees should also be reminded regularly of the need to keep confidential the fact that the practice is acting for that client.

3.9.4 Social media

With the increased use of social media, employees need to be clear about what they can and cannot say and a prudent legal practice will have a clear policy about the use (or non-use) of social media. The reputational risks associated with the use of social media are significant and given the informality of the media, it is very easy to fail to consider the implications of a brief statement.

The Law Society's practice note on social media may be helpful. There is a social media policy contained in the *Lexcel Information Management Toolkit* (2nd edition, Law Society, 2013) which may be useful as a precedent. Legal practices should ensure that if they intend to monitor employee activities, they consider the ICO's guidance on monitoring at work which is contained in the Employment Practices Code (available at **http://ico.org.uk/for_organisations/data_protection/ topic_guides/~/media/documents/library/Data_Protection/Detailed_specialist_ guides/the_employment_practices_code.pdf**). In addition, legal practices should take account of the human rights of employees as exemplified in the European Court of Human Rights case of *Halford* v. *United Kingdom* [1997] IRLR 471.

3.10 Privacy by design

Legal practices, particularly in the current climate, will be considering how to provide new services and products to their clients. Privacy by design is an approach where privacy and data protection compliance are integral elements of the development process of those services or products.

If a legal practice is developing an online service enabling clients to track their matter through the legal practice's website, there will be data protection, confidentiality and money laundering issues to consider. If the DP officer is involved at the start of the project, the issues and risks can be properly considered and appropriate solutions found.

If the project team does not consider privacy risks at the start of the project, there is a risk that the systems will not be sufficiently secure or insufficient client data may be sought or that the ultimate cost is higher because it has been necessary to buy an expensive 'bolt on' solution.

A good compliance culture is one in which the expertise of the DP officer (or other compliance expert) is sought at the start of a project so that all the compliance issues are identified at the earliest opportunity and appropriate, commercial and practical solutions found.

Further information on privacy by design and a privacy impact assessment is available from the ICO's website (**http://ico.org.uk/for_organisations/data_protection/topic_guides/privacy_by_design**).

3.11 Using the toolkit

The standard paragraph on data protection from the Law Society's practice note on client care is included at **Annex 3A**. Legal practices will adapt the provisions according to their business model and for example, their approach to direct marketing.

Where a legal practice in compliance with para.4.3.3 of the Law Society anti-money laundering practice note, uses electronic verification to check the identity of clients, it is not necessary to obtain consent from clients, but they must be informed that the check will take place. **Annex 3B** contains a sample electronic verification provision.

The full list of Sched.2 and Sched.3 provisions at **Annex 3C** is designed as a reminder although the consent condition in Sched.2 and the explicit consent condition in Sched.3 will usually be the relevant conditions for clients.

The issues surrounding marketing are complex as there is a range of regulatory and legal requirements to consider which may not be obvious. **Annex 3D** provides a list of the relevant requirements at the date of publication.

Annex 3A
Terms of business provisions/privacy notice

We may use your personal data (as defined by the Data Protection Act 1998) for the purpose of client identity verification, the provision of any of our services, the administration of files and records, legal and regulatory compliance and the marketing and promotion of our services, as well as informing you of relevant news and legal developments. The information will be held in hard copy and electronic form.

Our work for you may require us to provide information to third parties such as expert witnesses and other professional advisers. Any third party to whom we disclose information about you will be under an obligation to keep your information secure and not to use it for any purpose other than that for which it was disclosed. We may also disclose your personal data to third parties from whom we are buying a business/assets or to whom we are selling some or all of our business/assets as part of any due diligence process. Your personal data may subsequently be transferred to such third parties.

We may also be under a duty to disclose your personal data as part of our legal or regulatory obligations. We may need to disclose data to third parties in order to comply with those requirements or to prevent fraud or money laundering.

In certain circumstances your personal data may be transferred outside the European Economic Area (EEA) where data protection legislation may not offer the same protection as within the EEA. If you would prefer that we did not transfer your personal data outside the EEA please write to the partner responsible for your work.

Where you are acting as an agent or as a trustee, you agree to advise your principal or the beneficiary of the trust that their personal information will be dealt with on these terms. Unless you inform us otherwise, by disclosing any personal information to us about the principal or the beneficiary, we will assume you have obtained consent for the use of such information on these terms.

You have the right to access personal data we hold about you on payment of a fee of [£10] and subject to some exceptions. If you would like to obtain this data please contact the data protection officer in writing stating what data you require. [It would be helpful if you would include the words 'Data Protection Act' or 'Subject Access Request' in the heading of your letter.]

If you do not wish us to process your personal data for marketing purposes or if you do not wish to receive marketing emails or texts, please advise [*name and contact details*] in writing as soon as possible.

Annex 3B
Electronic verification provisions

We may obtain information about you from third parties in order to verify your identity.

In performing these checks, personal information provided by you may be disclosed to that third party which may keep a record of that information. This will be done to confirm your identity; a credit check is not performed and your credit rating will be unaffected.

All information provided by you will be treated securely and strictly in accordance with the Data Protection Act 1998.

[We will not undertake these checks without your consent. If you do not agree to these checks being undertaken, please advise us immediately. We hope you will understand that we will then decline your instruction. If you do agree to the checks being made, we require positive confirmation of your consent in writing. Please sign and date this form clearly at the end and return it to us by email or by post.]

[*N.B. there is no requirement to seek consent, you must simply advise the client that the check will take place. Some legal practices may prefer to seek consent.*]

Annex 3C
Conditions for processing personal data

Schedule 2 conditions – any personal data

- Consent of the client to the processing.
- The processing is necessary in relation to a contract entered into by the client or because the client has asked something to be done so he or she can enter into a contract.
- The processing is necessary because of a legal obligation that applies to you (except an obligation imposed by contract).
- The processing is necessary to protect the individual's 'vital interests' (e.g. medical records disclosed to enable urgent medical treatment).
- The processing is necessary for administering justice.
- The processing is in accordance with the 'legitimate interests' condition.

Schedule 3 conditions – sensitive personal data

- The client to whom the sensitive personal data relates has given explicit consent to the processing.
- The processing is necessary so you comply with employment law.
- The processing is necessary to protect the vital interests of the client (in the case where the client's consent cannot be given or reasonably obtained), or another person (in the case where the individual's consent has been unreasonably withheld).
- Subject to certain conditions, the processing is carried out by a not-for-profit organisation.
- The individual has deliberately made the information public.
- The processing is necessary in relation to legal proceedings, for obtaining legal advice, or otherwise for establishing, exercising or defending legal rights.
- The processing is necessary for administering justice.
- The processing is necessary for medical purposes and is undertaken by a health professional or by someone who is subject to an equivalent duty of confidentiality.
- The processing is necessary for monitoring equality of opportunity, and is carried out with appropriate safeguards for the rights of individuals.

Annex 3D

Legislation on advertising

The following are the main statutory requirements and voluntary codes on advertising, relevant to legal practices:

(a) Data Protection Act 1998 and the Data Protection (Conditions under Paragraph 3 of Part II of Schedule 1) Order 2000 (SI 2000/185).

(b) Privacy and Electronic Communications (EC Directive) Regulations 2003 (SI 2003/2426) as amended.

(c) E-Commerce Directive (2000/31/EC) and the Electronic Commerce (EC Directive) Regulations 2002 (SI 2002/2013).

(d) Business Names Act 1985, concerning lists of partners.

(e) Financial Services and Markets Act 2000 and the Financial Services and Markets Act (Financial Promotion) Order 2005 (SI 2005/1529).

(f) Consumer Credit Act 1974 (as amended), Consumer Credit Advertisements Regulations 2004 (SI 2004/1484) (as amended), Consumer Credit (Exempt Advertisements) Order 1985 (SI 1985/621).

(g) Companies (Trading Disclosures) Regulations 2008 (SI 2008/495) regarding the appearance of the company name and other particulars on stationery, etc.

(h) Consumer Protection Act 1987 and the Consumer Protection from Unfair Trading Regulations 2008 (SI 2008/1277).

(i) Unfair Contract Terms Act 1977 and the Unfair Terms in Consumer Contracts Regulations 1999 (SI 1999/2083).

(j) Business Protection from Misleading Marketing Regulations 2008 (SI 2008/1276).

(k) Committee of Advertising Practice Code and the UK Code of Broadcast Advertising.

Legal practices should also be aware of other regulations which may affect their relationship with their client, including the Consumer Protection (Distance Selling) Regulations 2000 (SI 2000/2334), the Cancellation of Contracts made in a Consumer's Home or Place of Work etc. Regulations 2008 (SI 2008/1816) (Doorstep Selling Regulations), the Provision of Services Regulations 2009 (SI 2009/2999) and the Financial Services and Markets (Distance Marketing) Regulations 2004 (SI 2004/2095).

4 Ongoing monitoring

4.1 Keeping data up to date and accurate

Under the fourth data protection principle, data must be kept accurate and where necessary up to date. Legal practices should take reasonable steps to ensure the accuracy of personal data, ensure that the source of the data is clear, consider any challenges to the accuracy of the data and whether the data needs to be updated.

It must be clear to all employees that data obtained must be accurately recorded and entered on the system. It must also be kept up to date so if the client notifies the legal practice of a change of address (ideally in writing) that information must be promptly recorded. Otherwise a letter enclosing a cheque may be stolen with a loss to the legal practice. There are also identity theft risks if personal data is inaccurately recorded.

4.2 Ongoing monitoring

In addition to keeping data up to date and accurate, ongoing monitoring of the client and the retainer will assist with data protection compliance.

If employees are unsure about any data protection issues relating to the client or the retainer, they must raise those issues with the DP officer at the earliest opportunity. Failure to do so could lead to allegations of a breach of the DPA and the risk of referral to the SRA or the ICO. Such allegations would affect the individual as well as the legal practice.

Legal practices should review the areas of risk and decide what systems and procedures will work best for the legal practice. Whatever systems are in place, employees must have easy access to the DP officer, who must be approachable, responsive, knowledgeable, commercial and trusted by employees.

4.3 Issues for employees to consider

Employees will be trained on the data protection legislation and their obligations to keep clients affairs confidential, keep information secure and comply with the data protection which should enable them to identify the issues which may arise during the retainer including:

- Subject access requests;
- Complaints;
- Data loss/breach;
- A data controller, data processor or a third party's use of personal data;
- Potential report to the ICO;
- Suggestions that data is inaccurate.

It is important that employees raise queries with the DP officer at the earliest opportunity to minimise and mitigate risks.

4.4 Discussions with the DP officer

Helping employees to identify the need to seek guidance is critical for the protection of the legal practice and its employees. The emphasis should always be on seeking guidance because making the wrong decision could have serious reputational consequences and/or result in a significant fine/enforcement action from the ICO and disciplinary action from the SRA.

The DP officer must be accessible and employees must know how to contact him or her easily, particularly if the matter is urgent. The DP officer will need to access the issues raised and give appropriate guidance on individual matters. The DP officer will want to record DP queries so that common themes and trends can be identified (see the DP officer query log at **Annex 4B**). This information will help you to identify training needs within particular teams and may also result in the DP officer drafting new procedures or amending existing procedures so that your systems are more robust and effective.

4.5 Using the toolkit

The ongoing monitoring procedure (**Annex 4A**) will set out the obligations of employees who will need to be made aware of the procedure and the importance of compliance.

The log of queries (**Annex 4B**) will be a valuable tool particularly if it becomes clear that a particular area of the practice is having operational challenges which might result in data protection incidents. Having early warning of a potential data loss will be critical and enable the DP officer in conjunction with the COLP to determine how best to deal with the issue, e.g. by making changes in the post room to improve the way in which outgoing post is handled or how faxes are sent.

A review of the log may show that there have already been incidents which seemed relatively minor but on further investigation reveal a more systemic problem. Legal practices may use the log as a subset of the overall incident reporting log.

If internal reports are made of data protection breaches, the DP officer will need to record those, decide what action needs to be taken, whether the breach is material (and so reportable to the SRA) and whether it should be reported to the ICO (see **Annex 5C**). As with AML issues, if a report is not made to the SRA, it may be prudent to make a note as to why it is not a material breach in the event of any further enquiries.

Annex 4A
Ongoing monitoring procedure

Purpose

[*Legal practice name*] is committed to compliance with its DP obligations, in order to mitigate the risks of failing to protect the personal data of clients or employees, breaching the data protection legislation or the obligations under the SRA Code of Conduct 2011.

This procedure sets out how [*legal practice name*] will ensure that ongoing monitoring is undertaken throughout the life of a retainer and general queries are raised with the [DP officer/deputy DP officer].

Application

[*Delete as appropriate:*]

This procedure applies to all employees in [*legal practice name*] including those undertaking work through a consultancy arrangement, in a volunteer capacity, on a temporary basis or through an agency. The term 'employees' is used to refer to managers and employees.

All employees must familiarise themselves with this procedure and comply with it. Failure to comply with this procedure [will/may] result in disciplinary action.

[This procedure applies to the DP officer, deputy DP officer, and all managers/ partners, fee earners and paralegals.]

Keeping information up to date

For all retainers, employees must take reasonable steps to keep client information up to date where necessary. This will include the following:

• Updating CDD information if there are changes, e.g. in identity details or address details.
• Updating information relevant to the retainer, e.g. changes about medical issues in PI cases.
• [*Specify other circumstances*].

These changes may occur between retainers or during a retainer.

[*Delete as appropriate:*]

[It is the responsibility of the fee earner to update the information.]

[It is the responsibility of the fee earner to notify the [MLRO/deputy MLRO/AML team] of changes requiring an update of the AML verification information as such personal data must be kept up to date.]

Steps must be taken to update the information within [*specify time frame, e.g. one week*] of the fee earner becoming aware of the change.

If the information cannot be updated within [*specify time frame, e.g. one month*] of the fee earner becoming aware of the change, the matter must be referred to the [DP officer/deputy DP officer] for a decision on what [*legal practice name*] should do to ensure the data is accurate.

Ongoing monitoring of a retainer

During all retainers, fee earners must stay alert to:

- indicators or risk of data loss;
- information which suggests that the CDD material or other information is false or otherwise incorrect;
- suggestions of any breach of confidentiality or of the data protection principles;
- potential complaints;
- breaches of the DPA.

[*Delete as appropriate:*]

[Where a fee earner notices any of these factors in a retainer, he or she must raise them with [his or her supervisor/the deputy DP officer/the DP officer] within [*specify time frame, e.g. 24 hours*].]

Where the [supervisor/deputy DP officer/DP officer] asks the fee earner to check information with the client, the fee earner should make those inquiries and make a note of the information provided.

Where matters are raised with the [supervisor/deputy DP officer/DP officer], the fee earner must provide his or her details and details of the client, matter number, type of retainer and nature of query.

The [supervisor/deputy DP officer/DP officer] must record those details on the attached form and provide appropriate guidance, including what advice was provided and when and how it was provided.

Related policy

Data protection policy

Glossary

AML	anti-money laundering
CDD	client due diligence
DPA	Data Protection Act 1998
DP officer	data protection officer
MLRO	money laundering reporting officer
PI	personal injury

Date of effect/date of review

This procedure shall come into effect on [*date*]. This procedure shall be reviewed annually.

Annex 4B

Data protection query log

Date and time	Fee earner/ department	Matter/file no. and client name	Query	Advice provided	Method of providing advice, date and time	Follow-up action/trends

5 Data security

5.1 What are the risks?

Legal practices are at significant risk from cyber attacks and security breaches, not only in relation to the data they hold but also as a route for hackers to access the clients' own systems. Legal practices hold a huge amount of confidential and sensitive information which is vulnerable to being lost through a lack of common sense/care and through ineffective or inadequate IT systems.

Regardless of the size of the legal practice, the seventh data protection principle means that legal practices must have appropriate security to prevent personal data (whether it is held electronically or in paper format) being accidentally or deliberately compromised. Failure to have effective systems can result in disciplinary action from the SRA, complaints and negligence claims from clients and the possibility of enforcement action or a fine of up to £500,000 from the ICO with the consequential reputational damage.

Principle 4 of the SRA Code requires you to act in the best interests of each client and outcome 4.1 requires you to keep the affairs of clients confidential unless disclosure is required or permitted by law or the client consents. Indicative behaviour 7.3 reminds legal practices of the need to identify and monitor a range of risks including IT failures and abuses, business continuity risks and claims under legislation, e.g. data protection. Legal practices also need to consider physical security issues, not only the risk of fire but also unauthorised access. Under indicative behaviour 7.4, legal practices must have arrangements to continue to provide services to clients in the event of an emergency, i.e. proper backup arrangements.

Increasingly, institutional clients will ask about cyber and information security, requiring practices to complete security audits and it is a relevant measure in panel reviews or legal practice selection generally. Practices that fail to show they are taking the issue seriously will have a real business risk, particularly given the increase in cybercrime.

Legal practices must ensure that:

- all laptops and portable devices are encrypted;
- data is kept securely and is only accessed by the right people;
- sufficient steps are taken to combat the risk of cybercrime;
- all IT systems are robust and there is a good business continuity plan in place, which is regularly tested;
- employees do not discuss clients' affairs in public or breach confidentiality;
- the right document is sent to the right person with the right enclosures at the right address;

- all data processors are clear as to their obligations and ensure that they handle data appropriately and in accordance with the arrangements set out in the contract.

Even in the best managed practice, errors will be made but such practices will have data protection/confidentiality and information security risks on their risk register, together with clear systems and controls to mitigate those risks and deal with those errors.

Legal practices should know what the risks are for their practice (see **Chapter 2**) which will include knowing what their assets are and what the threats are to those assets. Once a practice has identified both the assets and the threats, the practice should implement systems and controls to secure the assets, as well as implementing regular monitoring processes.

5.2 What systems and controls?

Given the scale of the challenge, this section can only highlight the major areas for legal practices to consider. Legal practices should also consider the practice notes on data protection and on information security, as well as the *Lexcel Information Management Toolkit* (2nd edition, Law Society, 2013). The SRA's guidance 'Spiders in the web' issued in February 2014 is also helpful and refers to the government's Cyber Streetwise campaign.

In addition, legal practices may find it helpful to consider the Department for Business, Innovation & Skills (DBIS) '10 steps to cyber security' guide and 'Small businesses: what you need to know about cyber security' (**www.gov.uk/government/policies/keeping-the-uk-safe-in-cyberspace/supporting-pages/providing-cyber-security-advice-for-businesses-and-the-public**).

'Cyber-security in corporate finance' published by DBIS and the ICAEW provides assistance to legal practices in tackling the cybercrime risks in corporate finance transactions (**www.gov.uk/government/policies/keeping-the-uk-safe-in-cyberspace/supporting-pages/providing-cyber-security-advice-for-businesses-and-the-public**).

Legal practices may wish to obtain specialist IT advice or obtain ISO 27001 although DBIS' new preferred cyber security operational standard, which is due to be finalised in spring 2014, may be more relevant.

Legal practices need to design and organise their security to be effective for the nature of the data held and the harm that may result (for the practice and the clients) from a security breach. The practice needs to be clear about who is responsible for ensuring information security, is it IT or the DP officer or both? The practice needs to have the right physical and technical security, backed up by robust systems and controls/policies and procedures and reliable, well-trained employees. The practice must be able to respond to any breach of security swiftly and securely.

All managers/partners and those in the business support functions need to understand the seriousness of the issue and promote effective systems and controls. The DP officer, the COLP and IT need to work closely together to ensure those systems and controls are appropriate and there is visibility of the risks facing the practice at all levels.

Your employees are critical because systems and controls are only effective if employees know what is expected of them and understand the importance of data protection/confidentiality/information security. Employees can be your greatest defence but equally they can be your greatest risk. Action Fraud (the UK's national fraud and internet crime reporting centre (**www.actionfraud.police.uk**)) recommends that businesses know their employees by undertaking pre-employment checks, having an anti-fraud policy in place and monitoring employee behaviour. The ICO estimates that 80 per cent of all data breaches involve employees in some way.

Employees need to be trained and reminded about the risks and issues such as confidentiality, IT security, not sending offensive emails, not giving out personal details and not opening spam or responding to phishing emails.

It is important to highlight that such emails can be quite sophisticated, e.g. scam emails appearing to come from both the SRA and the Law Society.

With the increasing use of social media both on behalf of the practice and at a personal level, a social media policy (**Annex 3E**) will make clear to employees how careful they need to be about the information they place on Twitter, LinkedIn or Facebook.

Other issues to consider are whether the practice has a clear desk policy, whether that is policed and whether visitors are able to wander around the premises, listen to conversations or see what is on a computer screen or a desk.

Fee earners should be reminded regularly about client-related risks, for example:

- confidential conversations must not be held on trains or in lifts (the very fact that the practice is acting for a client is confidential);
- confidential information must not be given to unauthorised third parties (e.g. the wife's best friend);
- ensuring faxes are sent to the right number at the right court and are collected by the right individual;
- client files/related documents are not left lying around in cafes, on trains, etc.;
- minimising the amount of information taken out of the office;
- laptops and portable devices are kept safe and secure.

Legal practices will need systems and controls to ensure:

- employees and contractors understand that client data must be kept secure at all times and what that means in practice;
- only authorised people can access, alter, disclose or destroy personal data and those people are only able to act within the scope of their authority;
- data is backed up securely;

- data held on laptops and portable devices, e.g. USB sticks, mobiles is encrypted;
- there are backup arrangements so if data is lost, altered or destroyed, it can be recovered to prevent any damage or distress to the individuals concerned.

Legal practices should also consider whether to allow employees to hold data on their own portable devices, e.g. mobiles, tablets, iPads, smartphones. The ICO's guidance 'Bring your own device (BYOD)' provides valuable information as to the advantages and disadvantages and what systems to implement. If employees are able to work from home, legal practices will need to ensure that personal information being accessed and used by homeworkers is kept secure. A recent investigation by the ICO found that the employer had no means of monitoring how personal information was being accessed and used and provided no guidance to help people working from home to keep personal information secure.

Increasingly cloud computing is an attractive option but legal practices should consider a range of issues, in particular, is it really secure and where is the data being held, is it in an unspecified jurisdiction? The SRA's guidance 'Silver Linings' (November 2013) and the ICO's document 'Guidance on the use of cloud computing' are helpful. The Law Society has also produced a practice note entitled 'Cloud computing'.

If the legal practice wishes to outsource any aspects of its legal processes, it will need to comply with outcome 7.10(b) of the SRA Code and satisfy itself that proper arrangements are made to protect client confidentiality. Where data is stored with third parties, e.g. archiving companies, there will need to be robust arrangements to ensure client data is kept secure not only offsite but also in transit (see **Chapter 6**).

Legal practices should ensure that their security measures are robust and cover the main issues. Further guidance is available in the ICO's 'A practical guide to IT security' (**http://ico.org.uk/~/media/documents/library/Data_Protection/Practical_application/it_security_practical_guide.pdf**).

5.3 Dealing with a breach of security or data loss

Legal practices may find that, despite the security measures put in place, a breach of security or data loss occurs. Legal practices need to deal with the security breach or data loss effectively, whether it arises from a theft, a deliberate attack, the unauthorised use of personal data by an employee or from accidental loss or equipment failure. Regardless of how the breach occurs, it is important to respond and manage the incident appropriately. Having a policy to deal with security breaches will be an organisational security measure demonstrating the steps you have taken to comply with the seventh data protection principle (see **Annex 5A**).

There are four important elements to a breach management plan (see the ICO guidance on data loss (**http://ico.org.uk/for_organisations/data_protection/lose**)):

1. Containment and recovery
2. Assessing the risks
3. Notification of breaches
4. Evaluation and response

Legal practices will determine whether the breach is material such that the COLP needs to report to the SRA. In addition, the DP officer will consider whether there is a significant breach which needs to be reported to the ICO.

Depending on the circumstances, the practice may also need to report the issue to the insurers and seek further advice as to the next steps to take.

Legal practices will ensure that their contracts with data processors set out the arrangements for security and what will happen if there is a data loss (see **Chapter 6**). The contract should be clear as to who makes any report to the ICO so that the processor does not make a report to the ICO without the legal practice's knowledge.

The ICO's Guidance on Data Security Breach Management is helpful as to how and when to report breaches (**http://ico.org.uk/for_organisations/data_protection/lose**).

5.4 Using the toolkit

Legal practices should have a clear policy for dealing with data losses/security breaches so everyone in the practice understands what they must do. Legal practices will need to adapt the data loss policy at **Annex 5A** so that it is tailored and appropriate to the needs of their business.

The checklist at **Annex 5B** will assist legal practices in taking all reasonable steps to implement appropriate security measures to reduce the risk of data loss/security breach in the future.

The procedure at **Annex 5C** sets out how to report to the ICO.

Annex 5D provides an internal form for reporting data losses/breaches to the DP officer.

Annex 5A

Data loss policy

Purpose

This policy sets out how [*legal practice name*] complies with the data protection legislation, confidentiality issues, information security and the SRA's regulatory requirements including outcome 7.5 and chapter 4 of the SRA Code of Conduct 2011, in the event of a loss of personal data.

Application

This policy applies to all managers and employees of [*legal practice name*], including those undertaking work through a consultancy arrangement, in a volunteer capacity, on a temporary basis, or through an agency. The term 'employees' is used to refer to managers and employees.

All employees must familiarise themselves and comply with this policy. Failure to comply with this policy [will/may] result in disciplinary action because of the significant risks of fines, enforcement action, reputational consequences and disciplinary action.

Seventh principle of the Data Protection Act 1998

Data controllers must take appropriate technical and organisational measures against unauthorised or unlawful processing of personal data and against accidental loss or destruction of, or damage to, personal data. Failure to do so can result in fines up to £500,000 from the ICO.

Responsibilities

All employees are responsible for ensuring that all types of data are properly protected and kept secure.

Data security breach or potential loss of personal data

If any employee become aware of any:

- loss or potential loss of personal data;
- breach or potential breach of confidentiality;
- loss of laptop or other device, e.g. smartphone or mobile phone (whether it belongs to [*legal practice name*] or to an employee personally) which may result in a loss of data or breach of confidentiality;
- breach of information security, whether physical or electronic;

the employee must immediately inform the [DP officer/deputy DP officer/COLP/ compliance team/supervising partner] so that appropriate action can be taken and because serious breaches must be reported to the ICO/SRA.

To enable the [DP officer/deputy DP officer/COLP/compliance team] to determine whether the breach is serious, the employee must provide the information [requested/set out in the data loss reporting form].

On receipt of the report, the [DP officer/deputy DP officer/COLP/compliance team] will respond to the incident.

Stage 1 – containment and recovery phase

The [DP officer/deputy DP officer/COLP/compliance team] will:

- investigate the breach [*and*] in conjunction with the COLP and the managing partner, [*and*] ensure they have appropriate resources;
- establish who needs to be made aware of the breach and inform them of what they must do to assist in the containment exercise;
- establish whether anything can be done to recover any lost data/limit the damage the breach [may/can] cause;
- identify any third party involved in the breach and liaise with them, as appropriate;
- where appropriate, inform the police and the ICO/SRA.

Stage 2 – assessing the risks phase

The [DP officer/deputy DP officer/COLP/compliance team] will assess the risks which may be associated with the breach before taking any steps after the immediate containment, as follows:

- What type of data is involved?
- How sensitive is the data?
- If the data has been lost or stolen, is there any protection, e.g. encryption?
- What has happened to the data?
- How could the data be misused?
- How many individuals are affected?
- Who are the individuals affected?
- What harm can come to those individuals as a result of the loss/breach?
- Are there wider consequences to consider?
- If an individual's bank details have been lost, what steps can be taken to prevent fraud?

The [DP officer/deputy DP officer/COLP/compliance team] will also consider:

- What are the potential adverse consequences for individuals?
- How serious/substantial are they?
- How likely is it that they will happen?

Depending on the conclusion, the [DP officer/deputy DP officer/COLP/compliance team] will decide who needs to be notified.

Stage 3 – notification of breaches phase

The [DP officer/deputy DP officer/COLP/compliance team] will consider the following in determining whether (and whom) to notify:

- [*Legal practice notice*]'s legal/contractual requirements.
- Will notification help to meet the security obligation in relation to the seventh data protection principle?
- Can notification help the individual?
- If a large number of people are affected or there are serious consequences, the ICO should be informed.
- How notification can be made appropriate for particular groups of individuals, e.g. vulnerable adults.
- The dangers of over-notifying.

The [DP officer/deputy DP officer/COLP/compliance team] will consider the following before deciding who to notify, what information to provide and how the information/message is to be communicated:

Who

- SRA (material or systemic breaches).
- ICO (significant breach/volume/sensitivity of data).
- Client/joint data controller/data processor/third party/insurers/banks.

How

- How to notify.
- How individuals can obtain further information.

What

- What information to notify.
- What steps have been taken to respond to the risks.
- What steps can be taken by, e.g. individuals to protect themselves.

If a decision is made to notify the ICO, the [DP officer/deputy DP officer/COLP] will report to the ICO in accordance with [*legal practice name*]'s procedure.

If the [DP officer/deputy DP officer] decides that there is a material or systemic breach, all relevant information will be passed to the COLP to decide whether to report to the SRA.

If the [DP officer/deputy DP officer/compliance team] decides that the client should be advised, [all relevant information will be shared with the COLP/the COLP will be advised of the circumstances] and the [COLP/DP officer] will decide how to advise the client and what information to provide.

If the [DP officer/deputy DP officer/compliance team] decides that a third party/ bank should be advised, [all relevant information will be shared with the COLP/the COLP will be advised of the circumstances] and the [COLP/DP officer] will decide what information to provide and what assistance to seek.

Any decision to report to the insurers (and what information to provide) will be taken by the COLP, in conjunction with the [DP officer/deputy DP officer/managing partner].

Stage 4 – Evaluation and response phase

The [DP officer/deputy DP officer] will evaluate the effectiveness of [*legal practice name*]'s response to the breach by considering the following:

- What was the cause of the breach/reason for the loss?
- What steps can be taken to prevent a recurrence?
- Was the response hampered by inadequate policies or a lack of a clear allocation of responsibility?
- Could existing procedures lead to another breach?
- Where can improvements be made to the systems and controls?

The [DP officer/deputy DP officer/compliance team] should ensure they:

- know what personal data is held, where and how it is stored;
- establish where the major risks are and why, how much sensitive personal data is held, is data stored across the business or concentrated in one location;
- consider the risks involved in sharing data with or disclosing data to others, whether the method of transmission is secure, whether the minimum amount of data being shared/disclosed, which data controllers/data processors/third parties the practice shares data with and whether the contracts need to be amended/ improved;
- identify weak points in the existing security measures such as the use of portable storage devices;
- monitor employees' awareness of security issues and address any gaps through training or tailored advice;
- consider whether to establish a group of fee earners/support staff to discuss 'what if' scenarios to highlight risks and weaknesses and provide an opportunity for employees to suggest solutions;
- implement and test a business continuity plan for data security breaches;
- identify a group of people responsible for reacting to reports of breaches of security or significant data loss.

Related policy

Data protection policy and related policies and procedures

Glossary

COLP   compliance officer for legal practice
DP officer data protection officer
ICO   Information Commissioner's Office
SRA   Solicitors Regulation Authority

Date of effect/date of review

This policy shall come into effect on [*date*]. This policy shall be reviewed annually.

Annex 5B
Security measures

Physical security

1. Are your offices secure, e.g. quality of doors and locks, protection by alarms, security lighting or CCTV?
2. How do you control access to your premises? When was this last audited and by whom?
3. How do you supervise visitors?
4. How do you dispose of paper waste? Is it shredded, onsite or offsite?
5. How secure are your archive arrangements, both offsite and in transit?
6. Are backup devices left unattended or locked away when not in use?
7. How do you dispose of old computers and multi-functional devices which will have data on their hard drive? Do you securely remove all personal data, e.g. by destroying the hard disk, before disposal?

Computer security

8. Do you have a well-configured firewall installed?
9. Do you have anti-virus or anti-malware products regularly scanning your network to prevent or detect threats?
10. Is your operating system set up to receive automatic updates?
11. Do you download the latest patches or security updates for your computers to cover vulnerabilities?
12. Do your employees only have access to the information they need to do their job?
13. Do you enforce strong passwords, limit the number of failed login attempts and enforce regular password changes?
14. Is all personal data held electronically encrypted?
15. Is the data on your computer system backed up regularly and kept in a separate place in the event of computer loss?
16. Do you have an anti-spyware tool installed? If not, would it be appropriate for your legal practice?

Email security

17. Is the content of your emails encrypted or password protected?
18. Does your email software have an autocomplete function? If so, make sure you choose the right address before you click send.
19. Do you use blind carbon copy to send emails to recipients without revealing their address to other recipients?
20. Do you check who is in an email group before sending the message to everyone?
21. Do you send sensitive emails from secure servers to insecure recipients, threatening security without checking the security of the recipient's arrangements?

Fax security

22. Do you consider whether it would be more appropriate to send information by means other than fax, e.g. by courier service or secure email?
23. Do you ensure that you only send the information required, e.g. if the other side asks you to forward a statement, only send the statement specifically asked for?
24. Do you double check the fax number you are using, e.g. by verifying it from a directory of previously verified numbers?
25. Do you check that you are sending a fax to a recipient with adequate security measures, e.g. ensuring that the fax will not be left uncollected in an open plan office?
26. Do you ask the recipient of a sensitive fax to confirm they are at the fax machine, ready to receive the document and that there is sufficient paper in the machine?
27. Do you call or email to check the whole document has been received safely?
28. Do you use a cover sheet to let anyone know who the information is for and whether it is confidential or sensitive without having to look at the contents?

Employees training

29. Do you train your employees:

   • so they know what is expected of them?
   • to be wary of those who may persuade or trick them into giving out personal details?
   • so they know they can be prosecuted if they deliberately give out personal information without permission?
   • to use a strong password (at least seven characters with a combination of upper and lower case letters, numbers and special keyboard characters, e.g. asterisk or currency symbols)?
   • not to send offensive emails about others, their private lives or anything that could bring your practice into disrepute?
   • not to believe emails that come from their bank or third parties asking for account details or passwords (and what phishing is)?
   • not to open spam emails, not even to unsubscribe? Ask them to delete the email and either get spam filters based on your computers or use an email provider that offers this service.

Annex 5C
Procedure for reporting to the Information Commissioner

Purpose

This procedure sets out how [*legal practice name*] complies with its obligations under the data protection legislation to report to the ICO.

Application

This procedure applies to all managers and employees of [*legal practice name*], including those undertaking work through a consultancy arrangement, in a volunteer capacity, on a temporary basis, or through an agency. The term 'employees' is used to refer to managers and employees.

All employees must familiarise themselves and comply with this procedure. Failure to comply with this policy [will/may] result in disciplinary action because of the significant risks of fines, enforcement action, reputational impact and disciplinary action.

Reporting to the Information Commissioner

Where the [DP officer/deputy DP officer] decides that a report must be made to the ICO, following compliance with the data loss policy, the following steps must be undertaken:

1. All information relating to the data breach must be collated to ensure that all relevant information is available.
2. The COLP must be advised and he will consider whether to report to the SRA at the same time. The COLP will advise the [managing partner/management committee/board].
3. A summary of the breach must be drafted, setting out the potential detriment, the volume of personal data lost/released/corrupted and the sensitivity of the data lost.
4. The ICO's data protection breach notification form must be completed providing full answers to all of the questions.
5. The completed form must be sent to casework@ico.org.uk with 'DPA breach notification form' in the subject field or by post to the Information Commissioner's Office, Wycliffe House, Water Lane, Wilmslow, Cheshire SK9 5AF.

[*Legal practice name*] will be contacted within seven calendar days of receipt to provide a case reference number and information about the next steps.

Related policy

Data protection policy and related policies and procedures

Glossary

COLP   compliance officer for legal practice
DP officer   data protection officer
ICO   Information Commissioner's Office
SRA   Solicitors Regulation Authority

Date of effect/date of review

This procedure shall come into effect on [*date*]. This procedure shall be reviewed annually.

Annex 5D

Data loss reporting form

Fee earner/ department	Name of client(s)	What was lost?	Personal or sensitive personal data	How was it lost?	When was it lost?	Likely impact	How was the loss discovered?	Where is the data now?	To whom has the loss been reported?	Lessons learnt

6 Data sharing

Legal practices will inevitably share personal data with other parties, e.g. counsel, other solicitors as well as suppliers and employees. The challenge is to identify what data will be shared, with whom and why and whether they are a joint data controller, a data processor or a third party.

Legal practices must explain to clients with whom their data will be shared, and why, to ensure compliance with the DPA and reduce the risk of complaints.

Once the legal practice is clear about the who, what and why, it should ensure there are robust systems and controls so that the data is kept secure, each party is clear about their responsibilities and knows what to do if there is any breach/loss. Given the SRA's requirements on outsourcing as well as the DPA obligations, the contract with the data processor should cover these issues.

The ICO's Data Sharing Code of Practice provides further assistance (**www.ico. org.uk/for_organisations/data_protection/topic_guides/data_sharing**) including whether the data sharing is systematic or whether it is an exceptional, one-off decision to share data.

6.1 Liaison with the data controller or processor

During the risk assessment (see **Chapter 2**), the legal practice should consider the following questions:

- Who provides personal data to the legal practice?
- Who receives personal data from the practice?
- Who is a data controller or a data processor (the distinction affects the respective responsibilities)?
- Is the data controller or data processor registered with the Information Commissioner?
- What is the nature of the data controller or data processor's business?
- What type of data is involved?
- Is the data sensitive personal data?
- Why is the data being held?
- What arrangements are there to keep the data secure?

The log of data controllers/data processors at **Annex 6A** provides a record of the controller/processor's details, the nature of their business, the type of data held and the reason for holding it, the security arrangements and the date of the agreement. This will enable the practice to have a clear picture of what arrangements are in place so that they can be properly managed.

Where the practice provides personal data to a data processor, the practice should undertake due diligence on the data processor before entering a contractual arrangement, primarily to ensure that the data is being kept securely.

Where data is received from data controllers, e.g. the NHS or Crown Prosecution Service, they will have their own protocols for handling and storage of the data and breach reporting with which the legal practice must comply. The legal practice must ensure relevant employees are aware of and understand the requirements and comply with those protocols.

Where the work of a legal practice involves another jurisdiction, e.g. in an overseas personal injury claim, the practice and the relevant employees need to become familiar with the particular data protection requirements in that jurisdiction. For example, a legal practice dealing with a PI claim in the US will need to consider the requirements of the Health Insurance Portability and Accessibility Act (HIPAA).

6.1.1 Data controller or data processor

Where the insurer receives details of the accident from its insured and passes that information to the solicitor to deal with the claim, both the insurer and the solicitor are likely to be data controllers. They are both likely to determine 'the purposes for which and the manner in which any personal data to be, or are to be, processed'. As joint data controllers, they will both have to comply with any subject access request (SAR) and report a significant breach to the ICO. The DP officer and the COLP will liaise about reporting to the SRA.

Where the solicitor obtains medical information from a personal injury client and passes that information to the expert witness to assess whether the client has a case, the legal practice will be the data controller and the expert witness is likely to be the data processor. The contract should set out the arrangements if either party receives a SAR, particularly to ensure that all personal data held by the practice and the processor is provided to the client to comply with the SAR.

Where the legal practice is the data controller, it will be responsible for the actions of the data processor and must ensure the processor provides sufficient guarantees about its security measures. The practice will take reasonable steps to check that those measures are put into place, have a written contract setting out what the data processor can do with the data and that the processor must only act on instructions from the data controller. The contract should remind the data processor that the documents should not be used for any other purpose or shown to anyone else, without consent, as the documents are confidential and so that legal professional privilege can be claimed where it applies.

A model data processing contract, published by the European Committee for Standardisation, is available at **ftp://ftp.cenorm.be/PUBLIC/CWAs/e-Europe/DPP/CWA15292-00-2005-May.pdf**.

Reports about significant breaches should be made by the data controller to the ICO. The contract should make this clear so the data processor does not report to the ICO without the knowledge of the data controller.

There may be circumstances in which the legal practice is a data processor, in which case, it will comply with the relevant requirements set out in the contract with the data controller.

6.1.2 Outsourcing

If the processing is being outsourced, the legal practice must comply with outcomes 7.9 and 7.10 of the SRA Code, bearing in mind the SRA's questions and answers on outsourcing, the SRA's guidance and the Law Society's practice note on outsourcing. Legal practices should be familiar with the SRA's Risk Outlook (July 2013), Risk Update (November 2013 and March 2014) and the SRA document 'Silver Linings: cloud computing, law firms and risk'.

6.1.3 Good practice

The ICO's Data Sharing Code of Practice suggests organisations:

- review what personal data is received from third parties, ensure the origin is known and whether there are any conditions attached to its use;
- review what personal data is shared with third parties, ensure it is known who has access to it and what it will be used for;
- assess whether any data will be shared that is particularly sensitive, if so make sure this data is given a suitably high level of security;
- identify who has access to information that third parties have shared and implement need-to-know principles so that only those employees who need to have the information are provided with access;
- consider the effect of a security breach on individuals and the practice (in terms of cost, reputational consequences or lack of trust from clients or third parties).

6.2 What type of data?

Legal practices will assess whether the data held by a data processor is personal data or sensitive personal data, as it affects which conditions for processing are relevant and the level of security required. An expert witness in a personal injury case who receives the medical records to assess, will be processing sensitive personal data whereas a mortgage broker who receives details of the client's financial circumstances to advise on a mortgage will be processing personal data.

6.3 Keeping the client informed

Clients should be advised verbally at the start of the retainer with whom their data will be shared, why and how that data will be processed, in the terms of business/ letter of engagement. The document should set out the position clearly and seek the necessary consent(s) which will reduce the risk of the client complaining that, for example, he or she did not realise that the judge would be provided with all of the medical information.

It may not be clear, at the outset of the case, that data will need to be shared with a particular third party, but the fee earner should provide the client with all the information as soon as possible. Treating the client fairly (see outcome 1.1 of the SRA Code) includes providing the client with all relevant information.

6.4 Security arrangements

Legal practices must ensure that the data processor will hold the data securely, to comply with the seventh data protection principle. The data processor must have security (physical and electronic) equivalent to that imposed on the data controller.

If a medical records agency outsources the pagination of records to a person working in his or her own home, the legal practice should ask what systems there are to protect that sensitive personal data. Is the individual registered with the ICO, are the premises adequately protected, is the data held securely, is the laptop encrypted and does anyone else have access to the data?

A data loss can occur through accident, deliberate destruction or damage. Having robust systems in place to minimise the risk of a loss and a security breach management plan will help both the data controller and the data processor to comply with the data protection principles. **Chapter** 5 (data security) provides further assistance on what to consider.

6.5 At the end of the matter

Legal practices should agree with the data processor what the arrangements will be at the end of the matter, either for the material to be returned or for it to be destroyed securely. If the data is to be returned, how will it be returned and to whom? Will it be sent electronically or by post? If it is sent electronically, is it encrypted or merely emailed? If it is sent by post, will it be sent by courier or special delivery or second class post? Will the data be returned to the legal practice or to the client?

The legal practice will consider the risks and decide how best to manage them. If there is no clear agreement with the data processor, sensitive personal data could be sent by the expert witness through the post to the client, creating risks of theft and identify fraud or distress.

If a legal practice can show to the ICO and the SRA that there are robust systems and controls to protect the data, then even if there is a problem, that should reduce the risk of any disciplinary/enforcement action.

6.6 Requests from third parties

Requests may be received from third parties for information about clients particularly under DPA, s.29. Those requests are likely to come from government departments or the police. Legal practices should have a procedure for dealing with requests from third parties under the DPA; a precedent for this is contained at **Annex 6B**.

Section 29(3) provides that personal data is exempt from the non-disclosure provisions if the disclosure is for the prevention or detection of crime, the apprehension or prosecution of offenders or the assessment or collection of tax. This exemption allows you to give out personal information; it does not require you to do so and the exemption does not override confidentiality.

Legal practices should not provide the information requested under s.29 unless the client has given consent. The usual response will be to advise the relevant person that s.29 merely allows you to provide information without breaching the DPA when a relevant exemption applies, but does not override confidentiality. You should ask for an appropriate authority (e.g. a production order) to provide the information or confirm that you can seek the client's consent. A standard letter to send to the third party is at **Annex 6C**.

6.7 External reports

Where the legal practice is the data controller, it will be for the DP officer to decide whether there is a serious breach which needs to be reported to the ICO. The DP officer is likely to liaise with any data processor to ensure that all information is provided to the ICO and that there is a co-ordinated approach.

Where there are joint data controllers, the parties are likely to report to the ICO jointly.

If the legal practice is both data controller and a processor for example, because it received medical records and then drafted statements, this will need to be explained to the ICO when reporting.

The procedure for reporting to the ICO is at **Annex 5C**.

The DP officer will also liaise with the COLP about reporting to the SRA. It is unlikely that there will be circumstances in which a report is made to the ICO and not to the SRA, particularly as the ICO may wish to discuss the regulatory impact of a breach with the SRA.

6.8 Using the toolkit

The log at **Annex 6A** should assist legal practices in identifying and monitoring the arrangements with data controllers/processors. Without clarity as to what arrangements are in place, it will be difficult to ensure that data controllers/ processors are dealing with clients' data appropriately and securely.

The procedure on responding to requests from third parties, e.g. government departments or law enforcement (see **Annex 6B**) should ensure that all employees know what to do, which will protect the clients and the legal practice.

Use of the letter at **Annex 6C** will ensure there is a consistent response to such requests.

Annex 6A

Data controller/processor log

Type of third party	Nature of business/ICO registration number	Type of personal data	Reason for processing data	Data controller or data processor	Security arrangements	Date of agreement				

Annex 6B

Procedure for responding to requests from third parties

Purpose

[*Legal practice name*] is committed to compliance with its DP obligations, in order to mitigate the risks of failing to protect the personal data of clients or employees, breaching the data protection legislation or obligations under the SRA Code of Conduct 2011.

This procedure sets out how [*legal practice name*] will ensure that requests for information from third parties are responded to properly by the legal practice.

Application

This procedure applies to all employees in [*legal practice name*] including those undertaking work through a consultancy arrangement, in a volunteer capacity, on a temporary basis or through an agency. The term 'employees' is used to refer to managers and employees.

All employees must familiarise themselves with this procedure and comply with it. Failure to comply with this procedure [will/may] result in disciplinary action.

Requests for information from third parties

The employee is responsible for transferring any telephone call received from a third party, e.g. a government department or the police requesting information about a client under the Data Protection Act 1998, s.29 to the [DP officer/deputy DP officer].

The employee will advise the caller that the call will be transferred to the [DP officer/deputy DP officer] and will then advise the [DP officer/deputy DP officer] of the name of the caller, the organisation and the details of the case.

If the [DP officer/deputy DP officer] is not available, the employee will take the caller's details and advise that the [DP officer/deputy DP officer] will return the call within [*specify time frame, e.g. 24 hours*].

The employee is responsible for forwarding any email or letter from a third party requesting information under the DPA or advising that a s.29 request is to be sent immediately to the [DP officer/deputy DP officer].

The employee will acknowledge receipt to the person requesting information, advising that the email or letter will be forwarded to the [DP officer/deputy DP officer].

The employee must not confirm or deny any information or indicate whether or not [*legal practice name*] acts or has acted in the matter or for that client.

The [DP officer/deputy DP officer] will, on receipt of the telephone call, email or letter, find out from the individual the key details about the case, what information is requested and the type of request.

The [DP officer/deputy DP officer] will advise the individual to whom the request should be sent and the relevant address, email and fax details.

The [DP officer/deputy DP officer] will, if it is appropriate, contact the [fee earner/ supervising partner/COLP] to advise him or her of the request, providing the key details and whether there may be any concerns at this stage about [*legal practice name*]'s actions in the matter.

The [DP officer/deputy DP officer] will consider whether to request the file from the fee earner or archive depending on the circumstances of the case.

Dealing with the request

On receipt of the request for information, the [DP officer/deputy DP officer] will assess its validity and provisions.

If the view of the [DP officer/deputy DP officer] [in conjunction with the COLP] is that the request does not override confidentiality, [he/she] will respond to the third party using the letter attached. The [DP officer/deputy DP officer] will usually offer to seek consent from the client to provide the information. If either consent is not forthcoming or the third party does not agree to consent being sought, the [DP officer/deputy DP officer] will explain that the information cannot be provided without an appropriate statutory authority, e.g. a production order.

If the view of the [DP officer/deputy DP officer] is that the request gives rise to concerns about the position of [*legal practice name*], [he/she] will take [internal/ external] legal advice.

The [DP officer/deputy DP officer] will be responsible for assessing whether and on what grounds the client should be advised of the request, and the implications and risks of doing so, usually following a discussion with the third party and, where appropriate, the COLP.

Consent from the client

If the third party agrees to consent being sought from the client, the client will be contacted by the [DP officer/deputy DP officer/fee earner/supervising partner/ COLP] explaining the request and the implications of agreeing to the request to override confidentiality and whether there are any grounds to agree to waive legal professional privilege. The client may need to be referred for specialist legal advice.

If the client gives consent to the provision of the personal data, the [DP officer/ deputy DP officer] will call for the file and advise the third party that consent has been given to override confidentiality (and, where applicable, legal professional privilege).

On receipt of the file, the [DP officer/deputy DP officer] will assess it and determine if there are concerns about the handling of the file and assess whether the personal data is subject to legal professional privilege/seek [internal/external] advice on privileged material, in conjunction with the COLP.

Where the [DP officer/deputy DP officer] is satisfied that the personal data is not subject to legal professional privilege, the data will be provided to the third party, retaining a copy for the practice's records.

Where the [DP officer/deputy DP officer] in conjunction with the COLP takes the view that the personal data is subject to legal professional privilege and therefore not subject to disclosure, a note will be placed on the file to that effect and the third party advised that certain data has not been disclosed as it is subject to legal professional privilege.

If the data requested relates to a third party, that data will be redacted unless consent has been obtained from that third party to provide the data.

The [DP officer/deputy DP officer] will liaise with the third party requesting the data to provide the data and deal with any subsequent enquiries.

Consent not sought or refused

If the third party refuses to allow consent to be sought from the client or if the client refuses to grant consent, the [DP officer/deputy DP officer] will advise the third party that the data cannot be provided without an appropriate statutory authority, e.g. a production order. If the third party serves a production order on [*legal practice name*], the [DP officer/deputy DP officer] will liaise with the MLRO and comply with the AML policy on responding to law enforcement requests.

If data is released as a result of being served with a production order, [*legal practice name*] will not breach the DPA by complying with the order.

Related policy

Data protection policy and related policies and procedures
Responding to law enforcement requests (AML) policy

Glossary

AML	anti-money laundering
COLP	compliance officer for legal practice
DPA	Data Protection Act 1998
DP officer	data protection officer
MLRO	money laundering reporting officer

Date of effect/date of review

This procedure shall come into effect on [*date*]. This procedure shall be reviewed annually.

Annex 6C
Response to a section 29 request

Dear Sirs,

Request for information under section 29 of the Data Protection Act 1998 (DPA)

I refer to your request for information under section 29 of the DPA dated [*date*], the contents of which have been noted.

I have considered your request and the relevant provisions of the DPA. Section 29(3) provides that personal data is exempt from the non-disclosure provisions if the disclosure is for the prevention or detection of crime, the apprehension or prosecution of offenders or the assessment or collection of tax. This exemption simply allows the provision of personal information in such circumstances without breaching the DPA but we are not required to release this information.

As a firm of solicitors, if we were to release such information we would be in breach of our duty of confidentiality to the client unless our client gave consent. Alternatively, if the information is requested under a statutory authority which overrides confidentiality, we will be able to provide confidential information. We would not be able to provide information subject to legal professional privilege.

We [can/will] contact our client and ask for their consent to provide the information requested.

Alternatively, please provide a court order requiring the release of the personal data or refer to a statutory authority which overrides confidentiality.

Yours sincerely

[*Legal practice name*]

7 Subject access requests

7.1 What is a subject access request?

A subject access request (SAR) is a request in writing from a data subject (e.g. a client or an employee) for a copy of the personal data held on the computer and in a 'relevant filing system'. The right is set out in DPA, s.7 and the sixth data protection principle.

The key points are as follows.

- A SAR must be in writing but does not have to be in a particular format. If a verbal request is made, a legal practice can respond if it is reasonable to do so and it is satisfied about the person's identity. Alternatively, it would be good practice to explain how to make a valid request.
- A maximum fee of £10 can be charged (unless the SAR relates to a special category, e.g. health records (see chapter 10 of the ICO's Subject Access Code of Practice (Subject Access Code) for more details **http://ico.org.uk/for_ organisations/data_protection/subject_access_requests**)). If it is decided not to charge a fee, it is not possible to charge a fee once a SAR is received.
- Ensure it is the right person making the request, usually by asking for evidence of identity. The level of checks should be reasonable bearing in mind the harm/ distress if it is the wrong person requesting the information.
- Information can be sought from the subject or requester:

  - as to the reason for making the SAR but the requester is not required to provide that information;
  - to enable the practice to find the data, e.g. if the request relates to emails, it is reasonable to ask for further details, e.g. a date range.

- Respond to a SAR promptly and in any event within 40 calendar days of receiving it. Failure to comply with the request can result in enforcement action from the ICO.
- A SAR does not need to contain the words 'subject access' or make any reference to the DPA.
- Even if the request is sent to a person other than the DP officer, it is still valid so all employees need to know how to recognise a SAR.

Legal practices should have clear policies and procedures which set out how a SAR is to be dealt with and by whom, so employees are clear about their obligations and the timescales. The training should emphasise the importance of recognising a SAR and passing it to the DP officer promptly.

On receipt of the SAR, it will be prudent for the DP officer to ask the fee earner/ partner what might have prompted the SAR, e.g. whether the client is seeking information prior to making a complaint. In that situation, it would be sensible to advise the complaints partner that there may be a complaint. There is usually a reason for making a SAR, although it may not necessarily be an entirely logical reason. Regardless of the reason for making the SAR, the request must be complied with but understanding the reason may help the legal practice to deal with any subsequent issues.

7.2 Will your employees recognise a request?

Legal practices must ensure their employees can recognise a SAR. Failure to do so can have serious ramifications for the practice. If the ICO receives a complaint about non-compliance, the legal practice may be subject to an assessment visit. That information will be shared with the SRA which is likely to consider whether the practice is compliant with outcome 7.5 of the SRA Code.

If the terms of business explain clearly how to make a SAR, it is more likely that the requester will use the terms 'SAR' or 'DPA' in the request, which is obviously preferable.

The ICO's Subject Access Code suggests that guidance and a form are made available on the practice's website, explaining:

- where and to whom the request should be sent;
- the fee and how to pay;
- the information that will be needed to confirm the identity of the subject;
- the 40-day period for responding to the request; and
- details of the point of contact for any questions.

The ICO's 'Access Aware' toolkit of materials can be downloaded and placed on display for employees. The key points are:

- if a client requests the information held by the legal practice about them, it may be a subject access request;
- a SAR does not need to mention the DPA to be a valid request;
- a SAR sent by email or fax is as valid as one sent by hardcopy;
- if someone asks you for the personal information held by the practice on him or her, it is your responsibility to deal with it;
- if a colleague asks you for the information the practice holds on him or her, it is a valid SAR;
- if you receive a request for personal information from a client or an employee, make sure you forward it without delay to the DP officer;
- effective handling of SARs will reduce complaints and the impact they have on the legal practice.

Clear messages and effective training together with regular reminders about the importance of compliance with the DPA should ensure employees refer any potential SAR to the DP officer immediately.

7.3 What systems do you have?

Your systems will need to set out how you will comply with a SAR from the point at which a request is received to the point at which the data is provided to the requester. The key elements are:

- the DP officer is notified as soon as a SAR is received, for example, in the incoming correspondence;
- the request is acknowledged and the fee banked;
- the 40-day calendar clock starts ticking as soon as you bank the cheque (which you must do promptly under the SRA Accounts Rules 2011);
- if the fee has not been received, it is immediately requested;
- appropriate evidence of identity is immediately requested;
- set out how you will collect the data;
- set out how you will ensure that data relating to a third party is deleted or redacted or consent sought;
- set out how you will respond to the SAR.

Individuals with a disability may find it difficult to make a SAR and if so, reasonable adjustments will need to be made, e.g. by treating a verbal request as though it were a valid SAR. If the request is complex, it could be documented in an accessible format and sent to the individual to confirm the request. You may need to respond in a particular format, e.g. Braille, large print, or audio formats. Legal practices must comply with chapter 2 (Equality and Diversity) of the SRA Code.

7.4 What data must you provide?

Legal practices must provide the personal data requested, unless there is an exemption. The subject's or requester's right is to see the personal data rather than a right to see copies of documents that contain his or her personal data. However, it will usually be easiest to provide copies of original documents.

The rights of the requester are to be:

- told whether any personal data is being processed;
- given a description of the personal data;
- told the reasons as to why it is being processed;
- given a description of the recipients or classes of recipients to whom data is or may be disclosed;
- given details of the source of the data (where this is available);
- given information about the reasoning behind any automated decisions taken about him or her, if requested (this is less likely to be relevant in legal practices).

The requester is not entitled to information relating to other people unless they are acting on behalf of that other person. The issues about third parties are considered in 7.5.

However, you need to be aware that people need not be identified as recipients because information is disclosed to them as part of an enquiry. This is to prevent an official investigation being compromised if an individual making a request is 'tipped off' about an investigation. Reference is made to the 'tipping off' and 'prejudicing an investigation' offences in the money laundering legislation.

There may be legitimate reasons for not complying with a SAR, so there are exemptions available (see chapter 9 of the ICO's Subject Access Code). If an exemption applies, you can refuse to provide some or all of the information requested. You are free to provide all the information requested: there is no obligation to use an exemption.

In considering the exemptions, a legal practice will bear in mind the obligation to 'treat clients fairly' and whether it is fair not to provide the information. Legal practices should also be aware that if an exemption is used, the ICO or a court could challenge the decision not to provide data to a requester. It would be prudent (and good practice) for the decision to be made by someone with suitable seniority (and expertise) and for that decision to be properly documented.

Clients may make a SAR, without realising they are entitled to the file, subject to lien. It may be easier to offer a copy of the file to the client and if he or she agrees, ask the client to withdraw the SAR. If the client does not do so, you must still comply with the SAR.

In complying with the SAR, the following points will be relevant:

- Is the information requested personal data? (See **Chapter 1** of this toolkit, chapter 5 of the Subject Access Code and the ICO's guidance 'Determining what is personal data'.)
- You must provide the requested information which is held electronically and any information that is held in a 'relevant filing system' (see **Chapter 1** of this toolkit and the ICO FAQs about relevant filing systems).
- You must, when collating data, consider what information might be stored electronically but which has been archived or backed up. Archived data must also be provided. The ICO's view is that if you delete personal data held in electronic form by removing it as far as possible from the computer systems, then even if it might be possible with expensive technical expertise to recreate that information, that does not mean that you have to go to such efforts to respond to a SAR.
- Emails should not be regarded as deleted merely because they have been moved to a deleted items folder. The contents of emails stored on your computer systems are a form of electronic record and will need to be provided even if it is difficult to find the data. It may be easy to overlook the obligation if the legal practice does not require employees to print off and file all emails.
- Where the SAR relates to data held at the time of the SAR but due to routine use, the data is amended or deleted while dealing with the request, you are permitted to supply the information as being accurate at that point. You cannot amend or delete the data if you would not have done so otherwise.

- If employees hold personal data on smartphones/personal computers, consider how you access that information. It may be prudent to have a policy restricting the circumstances in which personal data can be held on personal devices or in private email accounts. The ICO's guidance 'Bring your own device (BYOD)' suggests consideration is given as to whether to allow the use of personal devices to process personal data for which the practice is responsible. The practice will also consider the confidentiality issues.

While dealing with the subject access request can be challenging, it is important to remember that this right is fundamental to data protection. You should be prepared to make extensive efforts to find and retrieve the requested data and you are not permitted to exclude data from your response merely because it is difficult to access. You can ask for information from the requester to help you find the data but you cannot ask the requester to narrow the request. If someone asks for 'all the data you hold' about him or her, then you must provide that data.

Sometimes personal data can be difficult to retrieve and collate but that does not mean that you can delay dealing with the request. Dealing with a subject access request is time consuming and can be onerous, but a legal practice will need to ensure that there are sufficient resources available to comply with the obligation.

Once all the data has been found, it will need to be collated and supplied to the client in an intelligible (as opposed to legible) form. For example, any codes used must be explained but it would not be necessary to make poorly written notes legible, although it is good practice to do so.

7.5 Third party involvement

Legal practices will need to consider the different third parties who can be involved in a SAR and ensure that their systems and controls take account of the different issues:

- An individual or organisation may make a request on behalf of someone else. If that happens, you will need to be satisfied they have authority to request that information, e.g. by providing a written authority from that individual. It may be clear what authority the individual has, for example, because there is a power of attorney or a Court of Protection order.
- Where another organisation is processing data on your behalf, you may need to obtain data from that data processor in order to comply with the SAR. The client should have been advised to whom data will be provided (and why) at the start of the retainer.
- Where another person whose data forms part of the data is involved in the SAR, you will need to assess what data can be disclosed. You should not disclose data about another individual who can be identified from that information, except where the other individual has consented to the disclosure or it is reasonable in all the circumstances to comply with the request without that individual's consent.
- If a government department or law enforcement makes a request under DPA, s.29(3) reference should be made to **Chapter 6**.

7.5.1 Request on behalf of someone else

If a parent seeks information about a child, a legal practice should not simply comply with the SAR. Even if a child is too young to understand the implications of subject access rights, the data is still his or her personal data and does not belong to anyone else, e.g. a parent or guardian. The child has the right of access although, in the case of young children, those rights are likely to be exercised by those with parental responsibility. In responding to a SAR, consider whether the child is mature enough to understand his or her own rights and if so, respond to the child rather than the parent (see chapter 4 of the Subject Access Code).

If you think that the individual may not understand what information will be disclosed to the person making the request on his or her behalf, you may send the response directly to the individual rather than to that person. It would then be for the individual to show the information to that person if he or she wishes to do so.

If another organisation is making a request on behalf of another person, e.g. a solicitor, you will need written authority from that person, i.e. the data subject.

7.5.2 Data processors

If another organisation is processing data on your behalf, you will need to obtain the data from it to comply with the SAR. Sometimes it will receive the SAR which must be provided to you. (The contract should set out these obligations.)

The 40-day time limit cannot be extended because you have to rely on a data processor to provide the data requested.

7.5.3 Third party data

Legal practices should have clear systems for dealing with SARs which involve the data of third parties. Considerable care is needed to ensure that data is not disclosed inadvertently.

Although you may be able to disclose information relating to a third party, sometimes you need to decide whether it is appropriate to do so on a case-by-case basis bearing in mind your duty of confidentiality. You must not apply a blanket policy of withholding third party information. You cannot refuse to provide personal data about an individual simply because you obtained the data from a third party. Chapter 7 of the ICO's Subject Access Code suggests a three-step approach as follows.

1. Does the request require the disclosure of data that identifies a third party? Can you comply with the request without revealing data that relates to and identifies the third party for example by redacting data?
2. Has the third party consented? This is the best approach although it may not always be appropriate to seek consent if to do so would inevitably disclose personal data about the requester/data subject.

3. Would it be reasonable in all the circumstances to disclose without consent? Legal practices will consider this aspect very carefully as they may have a duty of confidentiality to the third party. Other factors to take into account are what steps you need to take to seek consent, whether the third party is capable of giving consent and any stated refusal of consent by the third party. In most cases where you have a duty of confidentiality, it will usually be reasonable to withhold the data about the third party unless you have consent.

7.6 Using the toolkit

Legal practices must have robust systems and controls to recognise and deal with SARs. Everyone in the practice must understand what to do if a SAR is received.

The DP officer will record all SARs on the log at **Annex 7A** to ensure compliance with the timescales and key requirements. While all SARs must be complied with promptly, it is important to record and ensure compliance within the final deadline of 40 calendar days.

The procedure at **Annex 7B** sets out how to comply with the SAR which will need to be tailored to the needs of the legal practice. The letter at **Annex 7C** is designed to be an initial response to the request. Standard letters of response can be attached to the procedure.

Annex 7A

Subject access request log

No.	Client	Fee earner/depart-ment	Date SAR received	Fee received (Y/N)	Fee banked (date)	ID requested and obtained	Reason for SAR, if known	Expires (date) (40 days)	Third party data?	Complied with

Annex 7B
Procedure for complying with subject access requests

Purpose

[*Legal practice name*] is committed to compliance with its obligations in order to mitigate the risks of failing to protect the personal data of clients or employees, breaching the data protection legislation or obligations under the SRA Code of Conduct 2011.

This procedure sets out how [*legal practice name*] will ensure that subject access requests (SARs) are handled properly in accordance with the legislation.

Application

This procedure applies to all employees in [*legal practice name*] including those undertaking work through a consultancy arrangement, in a volunteer capacity, on a temporary basis or through an agency. The term 'employees' is used to refer to managers and employees.

All employees must familiarise themselves with this procedure and comply with it. Failure to comply with this procedure [will/may] result in disciplinary action.

Receipt of a request for information/subject access request from a client

The employee is responsible for identifying that the request from the client is a SAR. The employee will receive training on how to identify such a request and will be provided with regular reminders about how to identify such a request.

If a client requests a copy of his or her file, the employee must contact the [DP officer/deputy DP officer] for guidance, who may decide to deal with the request on the basis that, subject to the lien, the client is entitled to his or her file. If that is the case, the DP officer will ensure that there is no suggestion that the client believes that he or she is making a SAR by asking for a copy of the file.

If it appears that the request is in fact a SAR, this procedure must be followed.

If a client makes a SAR, the [fee earner/secretary/compliance team/*other*] must immediately advise the [DP officer/deputy DP officer].

The [fee earner/secretary/compliance team/*other*] must check whether the fee of £10 has been received and whether there is sufficient information to identify the client.

The SAR must be logged by the [DP officer/deputy DP officer] showing the date on which the SAR was received, whether the fee has been received, whether there is sufficient evidence of identity, the department/fee earner, the likely reason for the

SAR and the date on which the 40-day deadline expires. That date will be diarised to ensure that [*legal practice name*] complies with its legal obligations.

The employee will acknowledge receipt of the SAR to the client using the letter attached [see **Annex 7C**], seeking further information as has been agreed with the [DP officer/deputy DP officer].

If the fee has been received, it must be immediately banked and the file noted accordingly. If either appropriate evidence of identity has been supplied or the [DP officer/deputy DP officer] is satisfied as to the identity of the requester, [*legal practice name*] must comply with the request promptly and in any event within the 40-day period.

If the fee has not been received, it must be immediately requested. If appropriate evidence of identity has not been supplied, it must also be requested. The period of 40 calendar days starts from the date on which the fee is received.

The [DP officer/deputy DP officer] will, if it is appropriate, contact the [fee earner/ supervising partner/COLP] to advise him or her of the request, providing the key details and to find out whether there may be any concerns at this stage about [*legal practice name*]'s actions in the matter.

The [DP officer/deputy DP officer] will liaise with the COLP and, where appropriate, the complaints partner where there may be a negligence claim or complaint following the SAR.

On receipt of the request, the [DP officer/deputy DP officer] will obtain the file from the fee earner or archive depending on the circumstances of the case.

Dealing with the request

On receipt of the SAR and the file, the [DP officer/deputy DP officer] will assess what information has been sought, whether all the information is held by [*legal practice name*] or whether information is held by a data controller/processor, whether the information requested includes data relating to a third party and whether consent should be sought from that third party to release the data.

If data is held by a data controller/processor, the [DP officer/deputy DP officer] must contact that controller/processor and ask for the relevant data to be provided at the earliest opportunity. If they are a data processor, they must provide the data. If they are a joint data controller, they may also be required to comply with a SAR. If the client serves both parties with a SAR, there will need to be close liaison in order to ensure full compliance and ensure all personal data is provided to the client.

If data is sought about a third party, the [DP officer/deputy DP officer] will consider whether the request can be complied with without revealing data that relates to and identifies the third party usually by redacting data. If this is not possible, consideration should be given as to whether to seek consent from the third party or whether the third party has already consented. If it is not possible to seek consent, the [DP officer/deputy DP officer] will consider whether it is reasonable to disclose data without consent bearing in mind any duty of confidentiality to the third party.

If a request is made on behalf of someone else, the [DP officer/deputy DP officer] will consider whether written authority is required from the data subject or whether the data should be sent to the data subject rather than the third party.

If the request gives rise to concerns about the position of [*legal practice name*], the [DP officer/deputy DP officer] will take [internal/external] legal advice.

The [DP officer/deputy DP officer] will be responsible for ensuring all the data is retrieved and collated, including emails stored on computer systems and other data, wherever held, e.g. on smartphones/personal computers. All employees must assist in the provision of such data, so that [*legal practice name*] complies with its obligations under the DPA.

The data will be collated by the [DP officer/deputy DP officer] and supplied to the client in an intelligible form. If any codes are used they must be explained; poorly written notes will be made legible. If the client has any queries regarding compliance, they must be addressed by the [DP officer/deputy DP officer] where reasonable.

Failure to comply with a SAR can result in an assessment from the ICO and audit/ enforcement action by the ICO or the SRA. Employees who are uncertain as to how to proceed must discuss the issue with the [DP officer/deputy DP officer].

Related policy

Data protection policy and related policies/procedures

Glossary

COLP	compliance officer for legal practice
DPA	Data Protection Act 1998
DP officer	data protection officer
ICO	Information Commissioner's Office

Date of effect/date of review

This procedure shall come into effect on [*date*]. This procedure shall be reviewed annually.

Annex 7C
Letter responding to subject access requests

Dear Sirs,

Thank you for your letter of [*date*] regarding your request for information under the Data Protection Act 1998.

We confirm we will comply with your request on receipt of the sum of £10.

Please also provide a copy of your passport and a recent utility bill so that we can be sure that we are responding to the right person.

Please would you also tell us why you are requesting this information. We would welcome the opportunity to find out if you are unhappy with any part of the service which we have provided to you. Please note that you do not have to advise us of this information but we would find it helpful.

Once we receive your payment and confirmation of your identity, we have 40 days in which to reply to your request. We will provide you with details of the personal data that we hold for you as quickly as possible.

If you have any queries about this letter, please contact our data protection officer whose name is set out below together with the contact details.

Yours sincerely

8 Complaints handling

Legal practices must have a complaints handling procedure and ensure that any complaints are dealt with in accordance with that procedure, as required by chapter 1 of the SRA Code.

This chapter considers the particular issues which arise if clients complain about how their data has been processed.

The potential areas of complaint include:

- How the legal practice has handled the personal data.
- How a data controller or data processor has handled the personal data.
- The practice has failed to comply with the information standards (data protection principles 3, 4 and 5) by holding more data than is necessary, the data is not accurate or up to date or data has been retained for too long.
- Data loss or insufficient security of data.
- The data has been passed to a third party inappropriately.

The sixth data protection principle gives individuals the following rights:

- Right to object to processing that is likely to cause or is causing damage or distress.
- Right to prevent processing for direct marketing.
- Right to object to decisions being taken by automated means (as this is unlikely to be relevant to legal practices, it is not considered further).
- Right in certain circumstances to have inaccurate personal data rectified, blocked, erased or destroyed.
- Right to claim compensation for damages caused by breach of the DPA.

Legal practices will need to have systems in place to deal with complaints about any of those issues and ensure there is appropriate liaison between the DP officer, the complaints partner and the COLP.

8.1 Duties under the SRA Code of Conduct

Complaints about data protection issues will be dealt with in accordance with the practice's complaints handling procedure but the DP officer and the complaints partner will have to liaise to ensure compliance with the DPA obligations.

Employees should be reminded that DP complaints must be dealt with in accordance with the practice's complaints handling procedure.

If a client makes a SAR, it may be a precursor to making a complaint and that information should be drawn to the attention of the complaints partner. Sometimes a client will make a complaint and a SAR at the same time, in which case, it is critical that there is close liaison between the DP officer and the complaints partner to ensure a coordinated approach.

The complaint must be considered carefully and the concerns properly investigated to determine whether the complaint has any merit. If there are any grounds which justify all or part of the complaint, then those issues should be followed up so that improvements can be made to the systems and controls, particularly in relation to data protection issues.

8.2 Right to object to processing

Individuals can object to the processing of their data but only if it causes unwarranted and substantial damage or distress, although they do not have that right if they have consented to the processing, or in certain other circumstances.

Clients will normally have consented to the processing so that the legal practice can provide legal services. Providing clear information at the outset of (and during) the retainer about how the data will be processed and the reasons for processing it, should enable the client to give informed consent to the processing.

If the individual does have the right to object to the processing of his or her data, that means he or she can require a legal practice to stop (or not to begin) the processing in question. To exercise this right, the individual must put his or her objection in writing and state what he or she requires the practice to do to avoid causing damage or distress. This is an 'objection to processing' or a 'section 10 notice'.

Further guidance is in chapter C1 of the ICO's Guide to Data Protection (**http://ico. org.uk/for_organisations/data_protection/the_guide**).

8.3 Right to prevent direct marketing

Clients have the right to prevent their personal data being processed for direct marketing (see **Chapter 3**). Your terms of business should make it clear whether data will be processed for direct marketing and you should have given the client the opportunity to opt out/opt in.

However, clients may opt in and then change their mind so they can, at any time, give you written notice to stop (or not begin) using their personal data for direct marketing. Anyone can exercise this right, not only clients, and if you receive such a notice you must comply within a reasonable period. (Although clients may seek to prevent processing where they are the subject of legal proceedings, it is unlikely that their data will be being processed for direct marketing. Such individuals may seek to object to processing on the grounds that it is likely to cause substantial damage or distress; see **8.2**.)

The definitions of direct marketing are considered in **Chapter 3**.

It is not necessary to respond to the notice, the obligation is simply to stop processing and there is no discretion about whether to comply. However, it is good practice to acknowledge receipt and confirm that the request has been complied with. Individuals may ask for their details to be removed or deleted from the database but, in most cases, it is preferable to suppress the details. This involves retaining just enough information to ensure that their preferences are respected in future. If their details are deleted, it will be difficult to ensure that the details are not put back on the database, at some future point.

8.4 Rights in relation to inaccurate personal data

Legal practices must take reasonable steps to ensure that data is accurate and up to date, where necessary. Clients (and employees) should be advised to notify any change of address or change of name in writing. Employees must enter data accurately into the legal practice's systems and if inaccuracies are identified, rectify them swiftly.

If letters enclosing sensitive personal data or financial data are addressed incorrectly, the client could suffer distress or financial loss. The legal practice could face disciplinary action from the SRA and enforcement action from the ICO.

It may be impractical to check the accuracy of personal data that an individual provides. Recognising this, the DPA says that even if you are holding inaccurate personal data, you will not be considered to have breached the fourth data protection principle provided that:

- you have accurately recorded information provided by the individual concerned, or by another individual or organisation;
- you have taken reasonable steps in the circumstances to ensure the accuracy of the information; and
- if the individual has challenged the accuracy of the information, this is clear to those accessing it.

It is important to ensure that all employees understand the requirements of the DPA in relation to the accuracy of personal data.

Employees should be aware that if data is inaccurate, the client has the right to apply to the court for an order to rectify, block, erase or destroy the inaccurate information. Therefore, any suggestion of inaccuracy needs to be addressed quickly. If the court does order that the data be rectified, erased, etc. it can also order that any third parties to whom information has been disclosed, be notified of the rectification, etc.

8.5 Right to claim compensation

Individuals are entitled to claim compensation if they suffer damage because of a breach of the DPA. There are also other remedies available to clients, e.g. to make a complaint under the complaints procedure and ultimately to the Legal Ombudsman (LeO).

The DPA does not define 'damage' but if an individual suffers financial loss because of a breach, they are likely to be entitled to compensation. Breaches may not cause financial loss but may be distressing. Distress alone is unlikely to be sufficient to entitle a client to compensation; however, if a client does suffer damage, any compensation may take into account the level of any associated distress.

The claim can be defended if there has been no breach of the DPA. Even if there has been a breach, the claim can be defended if it can be shown that such care was taken as was reasonably required in the circumstances to comply with the DPA. The defence is likely to include details of the steps taken to prevent any problems reoccurring.

8.6 Using the toolkit

The procedure for dealing with DPA complaints (see **Annex 8A**) will ensure that all complaints are dealt with in conjunction with the complaints partner and the relevant issues are addressed.

Annex 8A
DPA complaints policy

Purpose

[*Legal practice name*] is committed to compliance with its DP obligations in order to mitigate the risks of failing to protect the personal data of clients and employees, breaching the data protection legislation or the obligations under the SRA Code of Conduct 2011.

Application

This policy applies to all employees in [*legal practice name*] including those undertaking work through a consultancy arrangement, in a volunteer capacity, on a temporary basis or through an agency. The term 'employees' is used to refer to managers and employees.

All employees must familiarise themselves with this policy and comply with it. Failure to comply with this policy [will/may] result in disciplinary action.

Receipt of a complaint

If a complaint is received from an individual which makes reference to the DPA or:

- about how his or her personal data has been handled, including suggestions that more data has been held than necessary, the data is not accurate or up to date or has been retained for too long;
- about how a third party has handled his or her personal data or that the data has been passed to a third party inappropriately;
- suggestions of data loss or insufficient security of data;
- reference to the following rights:

  - right to object to processing that is likely to cause or is causing damage or distress;
  - right to prevent processing for direct marketing;
  - right to have inaccurate personal data rectified, blocked, erased or destroyed;
  - right to claim compensation for damages caused by breach of the DPA;

it must immediately be referred to the [DP officer/deputy DP officer] and copied to the complaints partner.

Employees must seek guidance from the [DP officer/deputy DP officer] if the client indicates any concern about how his or her data has been processed.

Dealing with a complaint

Any complaint relating to DP issues will be dealt with in accordance with [*legal practice name*]'s complaints handling procedure. The complaints partner will liaise with the [DP officer/deputy DP officer] to ensure that the DPA obligations are complied with.

DPA obligations

The [DPA officer/deputy DP officer] will review the complaint and assess whether [*legal practice name*] has complied with its DPA obligations or whether there is any merit to the complaint. The [DPA officer/deputy DP officer] will seek internal/ external legal advice, as appropriate.

The [DPA officer/deputy DP officer] will assist the complaints partner to respond to the complaint.

The [DPA officer/deputy DP officer], the complaints partner and the COLP will determine whether any follow-up action is required or whether there need to be any changes to [*legal practice name*]'s policies and procedures.

Related policies

- Complaints handling policy and procedure
- Data protection policy and related policies and procedures

Glossary

COLP	compliance officer for legal practice
DP	data protection
DPA	Data Protection Act 1998
DP officer	data protection officer

Date of effect/date of review

This policy shall come into effect on [*date*]. This policy shall be reviewed annually.

9 Data retention/destruction

9.1 Retention of data

Legal practices should already ensure that data is not kept for any longer than is necessary, in accordance with the fifth data protection principle. Clearly there are also commercial benefits to minimising the length of time for which data is held, given the cost of storage.

To ensure compliance, legal practices should:

- review the length of time for which data is held (whether electronically or in paper format);
- consider the purpose for which the data is held when deciding whether (and for how long) to retain it;
- securely delete data when it is no longer required;
- update, archive or securely delete data if it is out of date.

In practice, this means legal practices should know what data is held (see **Chapter 3**) and in which practice area. This will affect the length of time for which the data is held: for example, data relating to a child must be kept for longer than data relating to an adult in, for example, a conveyancing matter.

Legal practices should already have document/data retention/destruction policies in place and should be advising clients in the terms of business for how long files will be kept and how they will be destroyed.

However, while there may be systems to deal with files, legal practices need to ensure that there are also proper systems to deal with electronically held data. How will data be stored, will it be archived and will it be destroyed at the same time as the paper file? If not, what systems will the practice put in place to destroy the data? Retaining data indefinitely is unlikely to comply with the DPA so legal practices need to consider this particular challenge with their IT provider to ensure that the data can be deleted, if possible. Legal practices may be concerned about conflict checks but if no data (and no paper file) is held after a 10-year period, for example, it may be that any regulatory conflict is extinguished. A legal practice may take a view about acting where it becomes apparent that there may be a perceived conflict and consequential reputational risk.

The starting point is to decide the data retention periods, which will vary according to client and area of practice, as well as issues such as limitation periods.

9.2 How long do you keep it for?

Legal practices will continue to hold data for a minimum of six years after the end of the retainer. This will be for a variety of reasons, including limitation periods, VAT liability, regulatory requirements, e.g. Money Laundering Regulations and record of contact with the client. In some circumstances, data will need to be held for a longer period, for example, if the client is a minor.

The risk of claims or complaints is a very real one for legal practices. The ICO accepts that you may need to keep personal data to defend possible future legal claims but says that you could still delete information that could not possibly be relevant to such a claim. You should delete the data when such a claim could not arise. Reviewing the limitation periods will be important as well as the timescales for making a complaint.

The proposals in the EU Data Protection Regulation are likely to add complexity given the 'right to erasure' that is proposed. Legal practices need to balance the obligations under the DPA with the regulatory and legal requirements as well as the protection of the legal practice.

Legal practices should establish clear retention periods and implement systems to ensure that data is deleted at the right time. This will help legal practices to determine what data should be retained and when data should be deleted.

While legal practices may have systems to deal with paper files, they may not have the systems to destroy the electronic data, e.g. the information on the case management system including emails, at the same time. So it is important to ensure your procedure covers electronically held data and sets out the timescales for destruction and what data will be destroyed.

There may be different considerations for different types of data in terms of the length of time for which data needs to be retained; examples are:

- original documents, e.g. wills (see the Law Society's practice notes on file retention) – either indefinitely or for 50 years or returned to the client;
- paper files – at least six years but up to 24 years for a minor;
- emails – as per paper files;
- identity documents – at least five years under the Money Laundering Regulations 2007 (SI 2007/2157);
- client account records – at least six years;
- HR records (in relation to employees) – depending on the employment law requirements;
- internal audit reports – the legal practice will need to decide how long to keep these; these may include names of employees as well as clients;
- invoices – these need to be retained for accounting and VAT purposes for at least six years;
- basic client details (to show the relationship existed) – the legal practice will need to decide how long to keep such information and what details to retain.

When considering the data to be retained, the ICO suggests you consider:

- the current and future value of the data;
- the costs, risks and liabilities associated with retaining data;
- the ease or difficulty in making sure it remains accurate and up to date.

At the end of the retainer, a legal practice should have a system to review what data is held, whether it would be appropriate to delete any of it, whether there are original documents to return to the client and when the data should ultimately be destroyed. As part of this assessment, legal practices will consider the possibility of a claim or a complaint being made. If there appears to be such a possibility, a legal practice will retain the data/paper file until the possibility of a claim or complaint has been extinguished. The insurers may be able to provide further guidance on the issues to consider.

Legal practices will usually archive the paper files pending final destruction and should consider how to archive electronically held data at the same time, bearing in mind the practical implications to backups.

9.3 Destruction of data

The legal practice will have to decide on the process at the end of the retention period. The most prudent option will be to review the data before destruction, although this may be very expensive, particularly in terms of the staff time involved. A legal practice will assess the risks particularly in terms of which areas of work may be higher risk and determine what mechanisms to put in place to address those risks, for example, could an original document have been left on the file? Is there electronic data that had been overlooked earlier?

A legal practice may choose to have a longer retention period with automatic destruction but with the list of files to be destroyed being always signed off.

It will be important to keep the approach under review as there may be changes to the regulatory requirements which affect what data should be destroyed, for example, there are proposals in the fourth money laundering directive to reduce the amount of time for which CDD data may be retained.

Once the legal practice is satisfied that the data can be destroyed, it is critical that it is destroyed securely, both electronically held data and data in paper format.

How do you ensure that paper files and documents, including drafts, are destroyed: are they placed in confidential waste bins and then shredded? Is there a risk that confidential papers are simply put in the wastebasket for the cleaner to see? Robust systems will reduce the risk of data loss.

How do you ensure that electronically held data is deleted securely? If the data is deleted from a live system, is it also deleted from the backup system and the server? Legal practices will consider what steps can be taken to delete the data as far as possible, although it is unlikely that the data can be deleted completely. When computers and other storage devices are disposed of, are the hard drives wiped securely?

If a third party is used by the legal practice to destroy the files/data, what systems are there to ensure that the documents are shredded as opposed to being dumped at the local landfill? Are you confident that they are shredded securely? There should be a contractual arrangement with the third-party shredder which covers the outsourcing issues in outcome 7.10(b) of the SRA Code. The SRA has reminded legal practices about the risks of outsourcing.

In addition, it is not only the data the legal practice holds that needs to be destroyed securely but also any data held by a third party (see **Chapter 6**). A legal practice needs to be confident that the arrangements for data deletion are robust.

9.4 Using the toolkit

Legal practices need to have robust systems for the retention and destruction of data so that it is retained for the appropriate amount of time, reviewed and destroyed at the appropriate time and in a secure manner.

The ICO's guidance is also helpful in terms of issues for legal practices to consider; reference is made to chapter B5 of the Guide to Data Protection.

Legal practices may already have data retention/destruction policies in place. However the policy at **Annex 9A** may be of assistance.

Annex 9A
Procedure for data retention/destruction

Purpose

[*Legal practice name*] is committed to compliance with its DP obligations, in order to mitigate the risks of breaching the data protection legislation or the obligations under the SRA Code of Conduct 2011.

Application

This procedure applies to all employees in [*legal practice name*] including those undertaking work through a consultancy arrangement, in a volunteer capacity, on a temporary basis or through an agency. The term 'employees' is used to refer to managers and employees.

All employees must familiarise themselves with this procedure and comply with it. Failure to comply with this procedure [will/may] result in disciplinary action.

Responsibilities

All employees are responsible for ensuring that all types of data are properly retained and destroyed in accordance with this procedure.

Retention of documents/data

At the end of the retainer, the [fee earner/secretary/partner/*other*] must review the file and check whether any original documents are held. All original documents must be [returned to the client/held for [*years*]/held indefinitely].

The file belongs to the client, subject to a limited number of documents which can be removed and belong to [*legal practice name*]. Documents/data which come into existence during the retainer fall into four broad categories:

1. Documents prepared by [*legal practice name*] for the client and which have been paid for by the client belong to the client.
2. Documents prepared for [*legal practice name*]'s own benefit or protection for which the client has not been charged belong to [*legal practice name*].
3. Documents and letters written by the client to [*legal practice name*] where property passes to [*legal practice name*] on dispatch belong to [*legal practice name*].
4. Documents prepared by a third party during the course of the retainer and paid for by the client belong to the client.

The file should be assessed to identify which documents must be passed to the client on request and which should be removed and retained by [*legal practice name*].

The file should be assessed to determine what category the document/data falls into for document/data retention purposes.

The file will be reviewed to assess whether any documents/data are held by any third parties and what the agreement is with the third party is to destruction of the documents/data at the end of the matter. The [fee earner/secretary/compliance team/*other*] [will remind the third party of its contractual obligations [in the case of sensitive personal data/all personal data]/review whether any reminders are necessary].

Retention schedule

Type of document/client	Minimum requirement
Identity documents	5 years
Client account records	6 years
Client file, including electronic held data, e.g. emails	6 years minimum
Client is a minor	Up to 24 years
Basic client details	6 years

Paper files will be archived [*insert details of [legal practice name]'s archiving system*] and electronic data will be archived in [*insert details of [legal practice name]'s archiving system*].

Destruction of data

[At the end of the retention period, [archiving/facilities/*other*] will return the file/data to the [fee earner/secretary/compliance team/*other*] for [review/*other mechanism of approval for destruction*].]

[At the end of the retention period, [archiving/facilities/*other*] will check the list of files/data to be destroyed and pass the list to [DP officer/DP deputy officer/COLP/*other*] for checking and approval.]

[The [fee earner/secretary/compliance team/*other*] must review the file/data and check that there are no original documents. Any original documents must be dealt with in accordance with the document retention requirements.]

[The [DP officer/DP deputy officer/COLP/*other*] will review the list and assess the risks of any original documents being retained on the file. If the [DP officer/DP deputy officer/COLP/*other*] assesses the risks to be low or minimal, the [DP officer/DP deputy officer/COLP/*other*] will approve the list and confirm that the files/data are to be destroyed. If the [DP officer/DP deputy officer/COLP/*other*] assesses the risks to be medium or high, they will request the file and ensure that it is checked.]

In reviewing the file or the list of files to be destroyed, the [fee earner/secretary/compliance team/DP officer/deputy DP officer/COLP/*other*] must consider whether there is any possibility of a claim and if there is, immediately advise the [claims partner/negligence team/*other*] or any possibility of a complaint and if there is, immediately advise the [complaints partner/client care team/*other*]. In either case, guidance will be provided as to the steps to be taken, usually retaining the file for a further period.

[If there are no concerns, the [fee earner/secretary/compliance team/*other*] must send the paper file to [archiving team/facilities/*other*] for secure destruction by [internal arrangements/external arrangements]. The [archiving team/facilities/*other*] will notify [IT/*other*] who will delete electronic data consisting of [emails/*other records*] from the [case management system/*other systems*].]

[The basic details about the client will be retained electronically for [*years*]/All details about the client will be deleted.]

Related policy

Data protection policy

Glossary

COLP   compliance officer for legal practice
DP   data protection
DP officer   data protection officer

Date of effect/date of review

This procedure shall come into effect on [*date*]. This procedure shall be reviewed annually.

PART 3
Making sure it all works

The legal practice will have set up the overall systems as envisaged by Parts 1 and 2 of this toolkit. This section of the toolkit focuses on ensuring that employees understand their obligations and comply with those systems so the legal practice can demonstrate compliance with the data protection, confidentiality and information security requirements.

10 Training

10.1 Why train?

Under chapter 7 of the SRA Code, legal practices must train employees (outcome 7.6) and the practice and all employees must comply with data protection legislation (outcome 7.5).

A failure to provide appropriate training to enable employees to understand their obligations under the DPA and how to comply with the systems and procedures of the legal practice leaves the practice open to SRA/Solicitors Disciplinary Tribunal sanction, a fine and enforcement action from the ICO as well as significant reputational consequences.

It must be clear to all employees that they must undertake the training and on time. Failure to participate is likely to result in disciplinary action and may have an impact on performance reviews, appraisal and salary.

It must also be clear to employees that if they are unsure how to comply with the procedures and policies, they must seek guidance or further training to ensure that they can comply.

10.2 Who to train?

All employees should be trained on data protection, information security and confidentiality issues, regardless of seniority or position because their actions can adversely impact the legal practice. All employees are at risk of disciplinary sanction from the SRA so they must understand they are working in a legal practice and what that means.

If the office junior tells a friend that a famous footballer has been to see the family partner, that is a breach of confidentiality and the DPA. Revealing the true identity of an author writing under a pseudonym is a breach of confidentiality. If employees are not properly trained, they may not appreciate the potential consequences of a breach of confidentiality.

Legal practices will consider the differing training needs of employees and whether a 'one size fits all' approach will work or if a different approach is required for different teams, bearing in mind the risk assessment (see **Chapter 2**).

Those working in personal injury need to be trained on how to handle sensitive personal data as they are dealing with medical records; those in the employment department are also likely to be dealing with a range of sensitive personal data (e.g. sexual orientation, trade union membership). Those in the conveyancing department will be dealing with personal data such as the names, addresses, financial records of clients but not necessarily sensitive personal data. Employees need to understand the differences between personal data and sensitive personal data.

Employees in the business support functions also need to understand the requirements of the DPA:

- Marketing will be dealing with direct marketing issues and whether a particular client wishes to be contacted about particular services.
- HR need to understand how data protection legislation affects employees, including the possibility of employees making subject access requests.
- IT need to understand the importance of information security and how it relates to the DPA, so they can ensure that the IT systems are sufficiently robust and effective, that proper encryption is in place and that there is sufficient backup/ business continuity provision.
- Accounts/finance will need training on general data protection issues so they keep financial data secure and accurate. If bank details are incorrect, it could lead to financial loss for clients and the practice.
- Operations/facilities staff need to understand the impact of the DPA on their work, e.g. reception staff must ensure that confidentiality is not breached in meeting rooms and the reception area and clients' privacy is protected. Those in the post room need to ensure that faxes are sent/received properly and that post is handled properly.

10.3 Training issues to consider

Legal practices should take into account their risk assessment (see **Chapter 2**) in deciding what training will be appropriate for which employees so that the training meets the needs of the legal practice and the particular departments or business support functions.

As the requirements of different departments vary, the training will need to be relevant to that department to have the maximum impact. HR/training should be able to help to identify the types of training available and to implement the appropriate solution.

The training should include:

- an explanation of personal (and sensitive personal) data;
- an explanation of the data protection principles;
- what information to give to clients so they can give consent/explicit consent;
- how to protect personal data;
- the need to keep data accurate and up to date where necessary;
- how to recognise and deal with a subject access request;
- how to deal with data controllers/processors/third parties;
- what to do if there is a loss of personal data;
- details of the legal practice's policies and procedures and how to comply with them.

There are differing types of training including:

- face-to-face training;
- online desk-based training;
- a combination of the above.

Face-to-face training enables employees to interact with the trainer which may mean that they are more engaged. The training can be tailored to the needs of the particular department, by the DP officer with the assistance of the head of department, so it is more relevant. Providing real-life scenarios and how 'it can go wrong' will help employees understand the potential implications for the legal practice and the client of data loss or breaches of security.

For some legal practices, online training may be appropriate, as a practice can identify what training has been undertaken and by whom. It can be undertaken at the desk so reducing the amount of time lost from fee earning. Learning management systems allow legal practices to:

- record the details of the individual, including his or her status, department, SRA number, date of joining, etc.;
- allocate different courses to different teams;
- report which individuals have done the training and their assessment results;
- report who has not done the training;
- send reminders to those who have not done the training;
- link the training system with the continuing professional development (CPD) reporting system.

A combination of approaches may work for some legal practices, perhaps online training to provide a basic level of training with face-to-face training focused on issues relevant to that practice area.

If the training is successful, the DP officer should see an increase in the number of queries and requests for help to improve the systems.

Legal practices should also consider other ways of keeping these issues in the forefront of employees' minds and keeping them up to date with emerging risks and developments in the common law. Circulating the latest blog of the ICO on encryption or details of the latest fine will help!

It would be prudent to make notes about your assessment of training needs, how they are being addressed and why the training has been assessed as effective. This will demonstrate to the SRA and ICO that you have systems in place, which may mitigate any action if there is a breach of security or loss of data.

The frequency of training will be a matter for the legal practice. However, given the profile of data protection issues, training every two years is likely to be prudent.

10.4 Records

Legal practices should always retain a record of the training provided, including the material used, for CPD purposes and to demonstrate to the SRA and the ICO the steps that have been taken to ensure compliance.

10.5 Using the toolkit

The training procedure (**Annex 10A**) will set out the details of the training that will be provided to the legal practice and this should be easily accessible to all employees. The training delivery log (**Annex 10B**) provides a record of the training; a copy of the materials should also be retained.

Annex 10A
Training procedure

Purpose

[*Legal practice name*] is committed to compliance with its DP obligations, in order to mitigate the risks of failing to protect the personal data of clients and employees, breaching the data protection legislation and breaching the obligations under the SRA Code of Conduct 2011.

This procedure sets out how [*legal practice name*] will train employees to minimise the risk of [*legal practice name*] breaching confidentiality, information security or the Data Protection Act 1998 (DPA).

Application

[*Delete as appropriate:*]

This policy applies to all employees in [*legal practice name*] including those undertaking work through a consultancy arrangement, in a volunteer capacity, on a temporary basis or through an agency. The term 'employees' is used to refer to managers and employees.

All employees must familiarise themselves with this policy and comply with it. Failure to comply with this policy [will/may] result in disciplinary action.

[This procedure applies to the [DP officer/deputy DP officer/DP team] and relevant employees in [*legal practice name*] as set out below [*delete as appropriate*]:

- All partners and fee earners
- All support staff
- All accounts staff
- All HR staff
- All marketing staff
- [*Specify other*]].

Training for the DP officer

The DP officer is responsible for ensuring that the [deputy DP officer/DP team] stays up to date on DP law and practice including updates from the ICO.

The DP officer [and the deputy DP officer/the DP team] will undertake formal training [annually/every six months] by way of attending seminars or networking groups or completing online training.

The DP officer [and the deputy DP officer/the DP team] will also subscribe to and read:

- the ICO's monthly e-newsletter;
- [*specify any other relevant publications*].

Provision of training to the legal practice

The DP officer is responsible for preparing a DP training plan for [*legal practice name*] [annually/every six months].

The [HR/training/learning and development] team is required to assist the [DP officer/deputy DP officer/DP team] in providing the training, recording the training and ensuring that CPD records are kept up to date.

[*Delete as appropriate:*]

[The training plan will be agreed with the relevant practice area managers/partners.]

[Formal training will be provided by way of seminars or online training to all employees (other than the DP officer [and deputy DP officer/DP team]) [every two years/every 18 months/annually/every six months].]

[Formal training will be provided by way of seminars or online training to all relevant employees as set out below:

Employee group	Frequency

Formal training will cover the types of personal data, including sensitive personal data, how to protect the data, how to keep the data accurate and up to date (where necessary), how to respond to SARs, how to deal with a data loss and other issues relevant to the legal practice and each practice area. The training will include the steps to be taken by employees to comply with the law in accordance with the procedures of [*legal practice name*].]

The [DP officer/deputy DP officer/DP team] is responsible for providing alerts to all [relevant] employees on recent ICO fines or other data protection risks for the practice.

Training will be provided to all [relevant] employees on induction and transfer between departments.

If a supervisor becomes aware of a significant gap in a [relevant] employee's knowledge, he or she will notify the [DP officer/deputy DP officer/DP team].

The DP officer may require any [relevant] employee or practice area to undertake additional DP training where he or she believes it is necessary to ensure compliance with DP obligations.

Responsibilities of [relevant] employees

All [relevant] employees must attend, participate in and complete such training and achieve the necessary pass mark as is required by [*legal practice name*] within the required timescale.

Failure to do so may be noted on the employee's performance review or appraisal and may result in disciplinary action.

Record of the training

Details of the training will be recorded for CPD purposes and to demonstrate compliance with the SRA Code of Conduct 2011 and to ensure employees comply with the requirements of the Data Protection Act 1998.

Training will be recorded on the attached form [and/or] in the Law Society CPD centre.

Related policy

Data protection policy and related policies and procedures

Glossary

CPD   continuing professional development
DPA   Data Protection Act 1998
DP officer   data protection officer
HR   human resources
ICO   Information Commissioner's Office

Date of effect/date of review

This procedure shall come into effect on [*date*]. This procedure shall be reviewed annually.

Annex 10B
Training delivery log

Date of training	Fee earner/ status	Department	Title of training	Type of training (e.g. online)	Materials used (e.g. handouts)	Trainer	Summary of test results (pass/fail)

11   Monitoring compliance

11.1 Why monitor compliance?

Monitoring compliance enables legal practices to assess whether the DP policies and procedures are being complied with and are effective. The COLP and the DP officer should ensure that the DP monitoring programme fits with the overall monitoring programme of the legal practice.

Legal practices should ensure the monitoring programme is appropriate and proportionate to that legal practice, taking into account the overall risk profile, size of practice and type of work undertaken.

The aims of a monitoring programme will usually be to:

(a) identify whether the current procedures are being complied with;
(b) ensure relevant employees are aware of and understand the procedures;
(c) identify any compliance failings;
(d) identify any gaps in procedures;
(e) identify corrective actions;
(f) communicate the issues to the relevant people, e.g. the COLP, management board, supervising partner;
(g) ensure follow-up actions and improvements to the systems are undertaken.

The results of the monitoring programme will enable the legal practice to update the risk register and add any new issues to the legal practice's compliance plan.

11.2 Compliance monitoring programme

Legal practices will need to identify what the key elements of their monitoring programme will be and summarise the monitoring procedure so all employees know what will be monitored.

A compliance monitoring programme may include a review of:

- file reviews or internal audits;
- file checklist completion;
- the DP officer's log of queries;
- incidents/breaches of DP procedures;
- data losses/breaches of security;
- rectification of those breaches;
- data processor/third party issues or problems;
- SARs received and how dealt with;
- any issues arising from SARs made on behalf of clients;
- requests from law enforcement;

- requests or correspondence from the ICO;
- reports from the DP officer to senior management;
- how improvements will be communicated to employees and added to the risk profile of the legal practice.

File reviews or internal audits will highlight whether employees are giving proper consideration to DP issues, e.g. by identifying sensitive personal data or a breach of security/data loss. Follow-up action can be taken to remedy any failures and tighten up the procedures.

Queries from employees provide valuable information particularly as to the level of understanding of the regulatory obligations. If the queries demonstrate a lack of understanding, appropriate corrective action, e.g. further training can be provided. By reviewing those queries, the DP officer will be able to assess where the areas of risk are likely to be and how to mitigate/address those risks.

When a breach/incident occurs, the issues will obviously be reviewed given the reporting obligations to the COLP (and to the SRA/the ICO) and appropriate action taken. However, by looking at the overall level of incidents, the DP officer should be able to see the 'bigger picture' and identify whether the systems and controls are working effectively.

The monitoring programme should review how SARs were dealt with by checking, for example:

- how quickly the SAR was referred to the DP officer;
- whether the fee earner/secretary realised it was a SAR;
- how helpful they/the partner were in enabling the DP officer to comply within the timescales;
- how the SAR was dealt with by the DP officer;
- whether there were issues, for example, about the accessibility of material, the interaction with IT and how efficient and quick the process was.

Requests received from law enforcement or other agencies should also be reviewed. Is there a standard procedure for responding to s.29(3) requests (see **Chapter 6**) and do fee earners know what to do? Have there been any problems with those agencies following the practice's letter of explanation that s.29(3) does not override confidentiality?

If the legal practice makes SARs on behalf of clients, e.g. in personal injury cases, review whether there have been any problems either with the request or with the data received as a result.

Individual problems with data controllers or data processors should be dealt with when they arise but reviewing those issues as part of the monitoring programme will help to identify any systemic problems, e.g. about contracts, the responsibilities of data processors, data security or liaison with the ICO.

Feedback and follow-up are critical to a successful monitoring programme. A written report can be circulated to relevant managers/partners, e.g. the supervising partner, setting out the corrective actions. The legal practice's procedure will cover the escalation process if corrective actions are not completed. The DP officer may need to take further action, e.g. provide training or revise procedures.

11.3 Annual report

By submitting an annual report to the board, the DP officer can show whether the DP systems and controls are operating effectively and if they are not, identify why not. The details of the report are for the legal practice to determine but to be effective, it should be tailored to the legal practice's needs.

The report should take account of the risk assessment (see **Chapter 2**) and the SRA's risk management documents, e.g. the Risk Outlook. The aim of the report is to review the effectiveness of the legal practice's systems and controls, recommend improvements and identify any new or emerging risks (which should be added to the risk register).

It is likely to consider the outcomes of the monitoring programme, i.e. whether there are any concerns about the management of risks and priorities, including whether there are sufficient resources to protect the legal practice.

The report should allow the DP officer to set out his or her duties, take stock of the year, plan work going forward, document key DP performance and risk indicators, record the policies that are in place and identify key issues that should be reported to senior management.

The management board should consider the report and take any necessary action to remedy any deficiencies identified in a timely manner. Documenting that the report has been considered will help to demonstrate the steps being taken by the legal practice to comply with outcome 7.5 of the SRA Code.

11.4 Using the toolkit

The procedure for monitoring compliance (**Annex 11A**) should be accessible to employees so they are clear about what is expected of them and to those conducting the monitoring so they know what has to be audited.

The compliance monitoring form (**Annex 11B**) provides suggestions of what to monitor. Legal practices will need to adapt the form to the needs of their business.

Annex 11A
Procedure for monitoring compliance

Purpose

[*Legal practice name*] is committed to compliance with its DP obligations, in order to mitigate the risks of failing to protect the personal data of clients and employees, breaching the data protection legislation and breaching the obligations under the SRA Code of Conduct 2011.

This procedure sets out how [*legal practice name*] will ensure that the effectiveness of [*legal practice name*]'s policies and procedures will be monitored.

Application

This policy applies to all employees in [*legal practice name*] including those undertaking work through a consultancy arrangement, in a volunteer capacity, on a temporary basis or through an agency. The term 'employees' is used to refer to managers and employees.

All employees must familiarise themselves with this policy and comply with it. Failure to comply with this policy [will/may] result in disciplinary action.

The [internal audit team/monitoring officer] will undertake the monitoring of the DP systems in accordance with the internal audit process and this procedure and liaise with the [DP officer/deputy DP officer/DP team] and the COLP.

Compliance monitoring

Employees must co-operate with requests from the [internal audit team/monitoring officer] to provide files and other information to enable the [internal audit team/ monitoring officer] to assess whether:

- file opening checklists have been completed;
- appropriate/sufficient data has been obtained about clients;
- data appears to be accurate and up to date, where necessary;
- data is not kept for longer than necessary;
- data has been processed properly;
- subject access requests (SARs) have been properly dealt with;
- breaches/incidents have been reported to the [DP officer/deputy DP officer/DP team];
- data protection queries/concerns have been raised with the [DP officer/deputy DP officer/DP team];
- reports about data loss have been made to the [DP officer/deputy DP officer/DP team];
- there have been any compliance failings.

Employees and managers/partners must respond promptly to additional requests for information and acknowledge receipt of the report from [the internal audit team/monitoring officer]. Employees and managers/partners must complete any corrective actions within [*specify time frame, e.g. one month*] of the report. Failure to respond promptly to requests for information, acknowledge receipt of the report or to complete corrective actions will result in a referral to the [DP officer/managing partner/COLP] for further action.

The [internal audit team/monitoring officer] and the [DP officer/deputy DP officer/ DP team/COLP] will review the internal audit results and decide what action is required to rectify any non-compliance. The [DP officer/deputy DP officer/DP team/ COLP] will consider:

- how emerging risks are added to the risk register;
- what amendments are required to the compliance plan;
- how improvements will be communicated to employees.

The [DP officer/deputy DP officer/DP team] will review all SARs received to see if there has been compliance with the procedure and whether it is working effectively. The assessment will include a review of the time taken to respond, whether there were any concerns about how the SAR was complied with and identify any trends, problems or risks.

Provision of report to management

The DP officer will provide a report to the [board/partnership/*other*] on [*legal practice name*]'s compliance with its DP obligations [*every six months/annually*].

The [board/partnership/*other*] will consider the report and take any necessary action to remedy any deficiencies identified within [*specify time frame, e.g. one month*].

The report will include an update on the following information for the reporting period:

- Training provided to managers/partners and employees on DP compliance and the names of any managers/partners or employees who did not attend the training.
- Any material changes to DP risk factors affecting [*legal practice name*].
- Number of retainers terminated as a result of DP issues or concerns/complaints.
- Number of any DP breaches reported to or identified by the [DP officer/deputy DP officer].
- Number of SARs received by the [DP officer/deputy DP officer].
- Number of external reports made by the [DP officer/deputy DP officer] to the ICO.
- Any response by the ICO to a report made and any issues raised or enforcement action received as result.
- Requests from third parties under the DPA for information.
- Discussions with the SRA relating to DP concerns.

- Civil claims or notifications to insurers regarding DP issues.
- Results of any file audits or other monitoring activities of DP compliance within [*legal practice name*].

Related policy

Data protection policy and related policies and procedures

Glossary

COLP	compliance officer for legal practice
DPA	Data Protection Act 1998
DP officer	data protection officer
ICO	Information Commissioner's Office
SAR	subject access request
SRA	Solicitors Regulation Authority

Date of effect/date of review

This procedure shall come into effect on [*date*]. This procedure shall be reviewed annually.

Annex 11B

Compliance monitoring form

Type of monitoring	Date of monitoring	Key results/ concerns	Follow-up action	Date completed	Annual report
Personal data					
Review of queries about personal data					
Review of queries about sensitive personal data					
Review of data controller/data processor issues					
File reviews					
Internal audit results					
Review of breaches/ incidents					
Review of data losses					
SARs					
Review of SARs received					
Review of how SARs dealt with					
Review of time taken to comply					
Issues of concern arising from a SAR					
Reporting					
Review of internal reports of data loss					
Review of external reports to ICO					
Review of trends					
Review of ICO liaison					
Record-keeping					
Review of records of incidents/breaches					
Review of records of SARs and s.29(3) requests					

Type of monitoring	Date of monitoring	Key results/ concerns	Follow-up action	Date completed	Annual report
Internal controls					
Review of systems					
Review of DP procedures					
Review of policies					
Review of audits					
Review of contracts with data processors					
Risk assessment					
Review of risk assessments					
Review of guidance requests					
Training					
Training delivery log					
Training attendance report					
Communication					
Review of communications issued					
Discussion of DP at team meeting					
Document destruction					
Review of document destruction issues					

Annex 11C
DP officer report to management

Executive summary
1. *DP structure and governance*
2. *Summary of business issues*
3. *Report on procedures and policies*
4. *Conclusions and recommendations*

1. DP structure and governance
1.1 Name of the DP officer, where based, employment dates and experience:
1.2 Name of any deputy:
1.3 Reporting lines and link to COLP:
1.4 Summary of DP officer's responsibilities including extent of any delegations:
1.5 DP officer functions, including responsibilities, resources (and whether sufficient) and any restrictions on fulfilling the role:
1.6 When the report will be considered and by whom in senior management:

2. Summary of business issues
2.1 Overview of the legal practice: • [*Numbers and types of employees, practice areas, types of work*] • [*Major areas of risk, with reference to the risk assessment of the legal practice*] • [*Client demographic/type*] • [*Types of data held and by whom, e.g. personal data/sensitive personal data*]
2.2 Key strategic changes which will impact on the DP controls: • [*e.g. mergers*]
2.3 Other operational changes or other relevant issues: • [*New services*] • [*New systems, e.g. IT*] • [*Implementation*] • [*Improvements*] • [*New offices*] • [*Mergers*]

2.4   Clients and processes for collecting data:

[What processes are used and by whom, e.g. central client inception team]

- *[Size and type of client base by practice area/team]*
- *[Changes in client base, e.g. increase in PI clients]*
- *[Summary of checks on data held, e.g. who, how, how often]*
- *[Procedures for data processors processing data]*
- *[Systems for ongoing monitoring]*
- *[Systems for ensuring compliance and monitoring compliance]*

2.5   Types of services:

- *[Range of services]*
- *[Jurisdictions in which the legal practice operates and the risks]*
- *[How the services are provided and the risks]*

2.6   Data loss:

- *[Numbers of incidents, breaches]*
- *[Causes of incidents, breaches]*
- *[Details of significant losses, costs (financial and other, e.g. reputational)]*
- *[Complaints as a result of data losses]*
- *[Liaison with insurers]*
- *[Corrective action taken]*

2.7   Information security:

- *[Who is responsible for IT/information security?]*
- *[How are the risks assessed and added to the risk register?]*
- *[What IT systems/controls are there to counter cybercrime risks?]*
- *[What business continuity arrangements are in place?]*
- *[How frequently are they tested?]*
- *[What physical access controls are in place?]*
- *[How robust are those controls?]*
- *[Is there a 'bring your own device' (BYOD) policy and is it effective?]*
- *[Are all computers and portable devices encrypted?]*
- *[How do you address the security risks for the legal practice?]*

2.8   Data controllers/data processors:

- *[Issues of concern, e.g. data loss, breaches of security]*
- *[Contractual issues]*
- *[ICO concerns, e.g. notification or liaison]*

2.9   SARs:
- [*Number of SARs received*]
- [*Response times*]
- [*Subsequent issues*]
- [*Review of systems to identify SARs*]

2.10   Complaints:
- [*Numbers of complaints received*]
- [*Reasons for the complaints*]
- [*Subsequent issues*]

2.11   Document destruction:
- [*Issues raised, e.g. with process*]
- [*Concerns about the contractors*]
- [*Failure to securely destroy data, e.g. by shredding*]

2.12   ICO assessments/enforcement action:
- [*Numbers and brief circumstances*]
- [*Lessons learnt*]

2.13   Record-keeping:
- [*Format and location of records*]
- [*Any material failures and corrective action taken*]

3.   Report on procedures and policies

3.1   Overview of policies and procedures:
- [*Availability of policies and procedures*]
- [*How policies, etc. are communicated to employees*]

3.2   Training:
- [*Summary of training policy*]
- [*Training statistics for previous year*]
- [*Training provided (and to whom) in the previous year*]
- [*Training for DP officer and senior management, where different*]
- [*Evaluation of effectiveness*]
- [*Proposed training programme for next year including any budgetary issues*]
- [*Challenges in providing satisfactory and effective training and proposed solutions*]

3.3   Senior management information:

- [*Arrangements for regular reporting, frequency and identifying to whom reports are made*]
- [*Scope and coverage of regular reports*]

3.4   Policies and procedures:

- [*Effectiveness of policies and procedures, e.g. results of internal audits*]
- [*Compliance failings*]
- [*Corrective action*]
- [*Changes to policies, etc. and why*]

3.5   Monitoring arrangements:

- [*Systems and controls to cover DPA obligations*]
- [*Monitoring of systems and controls*]
- [*Monitoring failings*]
- [*Corrective action*]
- [*Improvements to monitoring arrangements*]

3.6   Reporting:

- [*Number of internal reports/queries and by which practice area*]
- [*Reasons for not reporting breaches to ICO*]
- [*Number of external reports to ICO*]
- [*Reporting trends*]
- [*Proposed improvements to systems*]

3.7   External factors:

- [*Use of Law Society updates*]
- [*Impact of recent cases*]
- [*Use of ICO guidance, including the e-newsletter*]
- [*Proposed regulatory/legislative changes*]
- [*Impact of external factors on policy and risk management*]
- [*Proposed or potential changes to policies and procedures*]

4.   Conclusions

4.1   Overall assessment of systems and controls:

- [*Are they proportionate and comprehensive?*]
- [*Have they been regularly reviewed?*]
- [*Material control failures, liaison with COLP, issues identified and remedial action taken*]
- [*Effectiveness of monitoring processes*]
- [*Adequacy of resources*]

4.2 Recommendations for action:
- [*Priorities for remedial action*]
- [*Time frame*]
- [*Resources required*]
- [*Potential impact of no action*]
- [*Other recommendations*]